AIR MADNESS

Runways and the blighting of Britain

'When the downsides of traffic became apparent, it was far too late to do anything about it. Attempts by recent governments have been like trying to hold the tide back with a saucepan. We are at the point of making the same mistake in the air'

www.pulfordmedia.co.uk/ituri

Also from Cedric Pulford and Ituri

Eating Uganda (history/religion)

JournoLISTS: 201 ways to improve your journalism

Acknowledgements
Grateful thanks to the late Maurice Landergan,
David Gant and Helen Szamuely for their advice and
to Michael Brown for pointing out Schopenhauer's
essay On Noise, which is quoted in Chapter Three

AIR MADNESS

Runways and the blighting of Britain

Cedric Pulford

ITURI

. Copyright (c) 2003, 2004 Cedric Pulford

The moral rights of the author have been asserted

First published 2003 by Ituri Publications
4 Chestnut Close
Woodford Halse
Northants NN11 3NB (UK)

2nd edition 2004

ISBN (2nd edition) 0 9536430 5 0

Text set in Century Schoolbook 11 on 13 point
with headings in Rotis San Serif
by Book Production Services, London

Printed in Great Britain
by Lightning Source

Front cover photo (c) Austin J. Brown/aviationpictures.com

A CIP catalogue record for this book is available from the British
Library

Contents

'Looks like the Mayor has extended the congestion charge upwards'

From the (London) Evening Standard, 12 March 2003. Reprinted with permission

ONE
THE MONSTER DEVOURS ITS OWN

PLANES have gone live as an environmental issue. We always knew that aircraft are noisy and polluting, while flight delays are an unwanted reminder of Europe's ever more crowded skies with the inevitable safety questions. But the British government's plans, announced in December 2003, for a huge expansion of airport capacity has made the aviation issue urgent. This is about more flights, more runways, the destruction of homes, the loss of green fields. It is also about more air noise, almost everywhere, even in the heart of the country. It is about atmospheric pollution and enhanced safety fears.

Nor does it end there. Airliners are buses of the sky – and who wants buses when they can have taxis and cars? Behind the growth in commercial flying is a steady expansion of corporate and private flying. Even the flying car – the family Ford – may be moving from science fiction to reality. All these activities too have their environmental downsides.

The plane is following the car in its environmental effects. Aviation is where motoring was early in the last century – and look what happened then! The car has moved from curiosity to chaos, from marvel to menace. It got that way because demand was unconstrained until it was too late to do anything. The same future, despite brave words from the Department for Transport introducing its airport plans (see Chapter Four), awaits us in the skies unless we act to balance our need for travel with the broader issues of a healthy society. To understand what is happening in the air – and the role of the DfT in promoting airways – we must first look at the story of the car...

From the start the car stirred high emotions on both sides. Pioneer motorists who thrilled to the "shock of speed" and even revelled in the breakdowns and the frequent punctures were more than matched by the wider public, who resented the noise, the danger – and the dust. Britain owes its ubiquitous tarred roads to the car, and it is almost impossible to imagine the distress caused by motor vehicles raising havoc on surfaces intended for nothing faster than a horse and cart.

William Plowden, in his classic account of the evolution of the motor car*, quotes a witness who told a commission of inquiry that after a Sunday afternoon walk he returned home "as if I had come out of a flour mill". Another witness, living beside a road, found: "All the plants under glass were spoiled, all the flowers were spoiled, all the strawberries and grapes were spoiled, and our health was injured. I had an inflamed throat all the summer and my eyes were very troublesome."

There were more major difficulties, like the deaths and injuries of other road users, or the intemperate speeds at which "road hogs" drove their vehicles, all fuelled by resentment of the "motor toys" of the rich. In the Edwardian dawn of motoring few imagined that these noisy, smelly, uncomfortable and unreliable machines would in the course of the 20th century become universal. They would become objects of desire far transcending utilitarian travel purposes. Millions would be married to their motor cars, which, however, would be lover as well as wife.

With the car humanity did not discover a whole new set of desires and satisfactions. Speed of travel had led

* *The Motor Car and Politics 1896-1970* (The Bodley Head, 1971)

those who could afford them to run carriages. Young men loved to try conclusions on galloping horses. The carriage provided privacy and, at least compared with the carrier's cart, comfort. But carriages were rare ... just how rare is suggested in Henry Fielding's *Amelia* (1751): the hero as a humble tenant farmer indulges his desire for a carriage. His richer neighbours consider this such an outrageous example of getting above oneself that they boycott him and start the downfall that leads to prison.

The motor car opened up the countryside for leisure and for living. In his autobiography, Rudyard Kipling told how in 1902 he bought Batemans cheaply because the previous owner thought it was too far (four miles/6 1/2 km) from a railway station. When told that Kipling would be using his Lanchester "contraption", the vendor said, "Oh, those things haven't come to stay." Years later the man acknowledged that he should have charged twice the price for the house*.

So the car emerged upon a waiting world. It promised to satisfy those desires even more than the private carriages did. The question was whether the car could develop mechanically from a toy to a tool. Nor could the thinkers of the time have foreseen the mass production that would finally put a car within reach of almost everybody.

Just as the car satisfied desires more thoroughly than the carriage – faster, more comfortable – so it has increased the downside – noisier, more dangerous, more polluting. The life-story of the motor car has moved from resistance to acceptance and back to resistance – if we accept as resistance the campaigning efforts of a small band of environmentalists and at least lip-service paid by most members of the public to the idea of restraining the car.

Until 1909 in Britain local authorities were responsible for maintaining the roads in their districts. Many

---

* Quoted by Peter Thorold in *The Motoring Age* (Profile Books, 2003)

ratepayers resented having to pay for the damage caused by through traffic. In that year, Parliament approved the creation of a Road Board, based on the principle of hypothecating (or earmarking) the revenue from motor taxation for the building, tarring and upkeep of roads. The Road Fund was to have a long and controversial history with the government proving unable to resist raids on the fund, but the immediate effect was to defuse the political issue of the car. Other problems, like noise, speeding and accidents, remained but it seems that the solution to road funding swept away the public's concerns. Plowden comments: "Even allowing for the other preoccupations of Cabinet and Parliament in the years after 1909, the disappearance of the motor car as a topic of political debate is striking."

In 1910, after more than a decade of motorisation, there were just 53,196 cars on British roads. They were about a third of total motor vehicles. The proportions were similar in the last year before the First World War: 132,015 cars out of a total 388,860 motor vehicles. It was to be 1932 before cars outnumbered other motor vehicles. By that time there were 1,127,681 cars out of 2,227,099 motor vehicles. In August 1939, just before the start of the Second World War, the number of motor vehicles was still extremely small by modern standards, 3,148,600, of which cars were 2,034,400 (less than eight per cent of the present total). Here was the time when the joys of the open, and by now well tarred, road could be savoured before other drivers came along and spoilt it all!

By the interwar years the car had moved "from a demon to a respectable citizen", in Mark Liniado's words in *Car Culture and Countryside Change**. Conservationists no longer sought to restrain the car as a threat to the beauty and tranquillity of rural England. The car, in fact, became the chief means by which the

---

* (The National Trust, 1996)

middle class could explore those beauties and tranquillities. Instead, conservation efforts were directed at restricting unsightly landscape and roadside developments including advertising. In 1929 the Shell oil company was persuaded to remove nearly 18,000 outdoor advertisements.

This relatively trivial environmental focus illustrates the fateful shift from resistance to acceptance that accompanied the spread of car ownership among the middle classes. Cars had ceased to be the perquisites of the rich. We are all more spurred to oppose what we can't have! Now that the car has become ubiquitous, greens argue that the monster has got out of control, that the disbenefits have outstripped the benefits. To have a chance of shifting Joe Motorist's mood, however, environmentalists have to face up to the pleasurable side of motoring, and take the debate on from there.

The car didn't get where it is by advertising alone, even though cars are by far and away the most expensive consumer goods promoted on television and one of the most repetitively plugged products. Advertising, which turns vague wants into compelling needs, cannot work its magic on inert material, where the seed of desire is not present. Cars offer freedom of movement, privacy and the pleasure of sitting behind a great deal of power on the open road (where it can still be found). For conspicuous display a high quality car is in the same league as diamonds and gold, but it can be brought out more often and seen by many more people.

These treasured attributes of the car are partly formed by the car itself, so there is a self-reinforcing spiral at work. For instance, the presence of cars has given us greater expectations of movement, and has also created a culture of privacy on the move (compared with the communality of public transport).

For rural dwellers, far away from the frequent public transport of urban areas, there is little choice. People need the car because they live in the country – and yet for the many who have moved to the country from choice they live there because of the car. Like the train before it, the car has transformed our expectations of where we may live.

In the 19th century railways created a class of travellers, later called commuters, who no longer had to live close to where they worked. On a daily basis they travelled from quiet and pleasant outer suburbs to their work in the noisy and unhealthy cities. In the second part of the 20th century the car took this process further, allowing commuters to penetrate even deeper into the countryside, using their vehicles to travel to a station and taking the train to town.

Thus there arose a disconnection between where we work and where we live, with many people either wanting or expecting to travel vast distances to their jobs. When the government was building new towns like Harlow and Stevenage in the Fifties and Sixties, it was already becoming too late for the integrated communities that the plans envisaged. Residential and commercial quarters, separate but adjacent, might be all very well but those who could afford it much preferred to live in picturesque villages and travel to work by car.

As personal mobility increased it was no longer necessary to have offices and factories in central urban areas well served by public transport. With the attraction of lower site costs or rentals, many offices and factories moved to the edge of town or even into the country. The last years of the 20th century were the era of the business park and the industrial estate. It might be a pleasant (if boring) environment in which to work, but a car was all but inevitable to get there.

Meanwhile, it became increasingly common for households to contain several cars. With several earners in the family, each needed a car to get to work. Car sharing with others in the same workplace held very little appeal. It meant a loss of privacy and flexibility of movement, two of the main attractions of the car. Driving myself to work I can play exactly the music I want, and I can come and go exactly when I choose. Few drivers were sufficiently hard pressed to need the extra money from car sharing.

Through shopping and leisure, the car has transformed the geography of the nation. Edge-of-town supermarkets and Aladdin's caves of do-it-yourself hardware would not be there without cars to carry the customers in and the goods out. Golf courses in the middle of the country depend utterly on the car, while stately homes and pleasure parks without the car would receive not hundreds of thousands of visitors each year but just a few coachloads.

The very shape of Britain has been transformed by the car. The pre-war city of Plymouth, with 250,000 population, had about the same number of people on half the land area of the city 50 years later. The compact cities and towns of the horse years have been replaced by spreading, not to say sprawling, urban areas. It is partly about replacing slums with decent homes but it is also about spreading property ownership and building wide not high. Why not when access to the centre no longer depends on our feet taking us there or on a tram at the next street corner?

Plot sizes before the Second World War were often extravagant, leading to the unpleasant ribbon development along the south coast that joins Poole to the Isle of Thanet and into the Thames Estuary with barely a break. Housing density now has greatly increased under threat of towns growing and running into each other – a position already reached on the American east and west coasts and in Ontario, Canada (and reached, too, in 19th century Britain in the Manchester, Leeds/Bradford and Stoke-on-Trent conurbations).

Local councils, however, are engaged in a constant line-holding operation, with pressure on green belts around towns and cities and demand-led directives from central government to find space for more housing units.

Growing affluence means an effectively infinite demand for housing in a finite area of land. Predicated on the personal mobility of the car, second and even third homes are within reach of more and more. At the start of the 21st century one of the most pressing social problems is that in many areas local people cannot afford to buy houses. Commuters and second-homers have pushed prices beyond the reach of local wages. Well-to-do retirees looking for a pleasant spot for their last years compound this complex process, but essentially it is powered by the car, allowing easy access for the incomers. Without the car the housing market outside the urban areas would settle at a level much more affordable for local people. Commuters would keep prices high in areas served by the train, but demand for second homes in areas like East Anglia and Wales would collapse.

It is not only local people who suffer from a distorted property market. First-time buyers are often priced out. The Halifax mortgage bank reported (May 2002) that first-timers could not afford to buy in more than a third of 451 British towns and cities. The least affordable places of all were London and popular suburbs and commuter towns like Sevenoaks, Richmond, Windsor, Winchester and St Albans. But the crazy prices uncovered in the Halifax survey go far beyond the big city effect of demand driven by popularity and scarcity: many smaller places suffer from unaffordable prices because they are popular dormitories – they are within easy commuting range by car.

So in the language of rights, your human right to live where you please and spend your spare money on what you please is in collision with my human right to live in the community where I work and where I grew up. Your human right to climb the property ladder clashes with my human right to get on it. Perhaps all of these are equally fundamental rights – or perhaps none of them are. Whatever the solution (and the small island of Jersey, for example, has found it necessary to bar most outsiders from owning property) we should start with the role of the car.

The consequences of the car for Britain's towns and cities were plainly set out in the Buchanan report, *Traffic In Towns*. This was published in 1963 after a period when the soaraway growth of private motoring had started to show itself. A character in A.J. Cronin's *The Northern Light* (1958) suffers a puncture while driving from a northern city to a nearby seaside village. While the puncture is being mended "Smith kept looking down the road, hoping for a car that might give him a lift, but the only conveyance that passed was the local bus going in the opposite direction". A few years later it would have been absurd to write about the road in those terms.

Between 1951, when the Conservative party returned to power and relaxed controls of consumer spending, and 1963 the number of cars increased fourfold – broadly, from two million to eight million. This transformation in mobility was very sudden, and few people expected it. From eight million car ownership has kept on going: the figure that stirred Colin Buchanan and his associates was less than a third of the present total.

The message of the Buchanan report – widely misunderstood as a crude plea to pull town centres to bits to accommodate the car – was that society must choose how it wished to cope with the car. Things could not go on as they were. That did not stop the authorities from hoping they could, and ignoring the strategic issues for many more years.

Much of the problem, as emerges from the 1992 report *Where Motor-Car Is Master*, from the Council for the Protection of Rural England (CPRE)*, was that for many years the Department of Transport had been in effect the ministry for building roads. (This is the department that is now deciding the future of our skies.) Its fixation with roads went back even further than 1936, but the Trunk Roads Act of that year was a turning point. It gave the then Ministry of Transport control of 4,500 miles (7,200kms) of national through routes, and the ministry itself became the builder of new trunk roads. "The fundamental significance of the Trunk Roads Act was that, by giving the ministry a direct executive responsibility for this one aspect of transport only, it inevitably resulted in an organisational commitment to inter-urban roadbuilding at the expense of an overall and balanced view of transport needs." Here is one of the roots of the imbalance that even today the transport department cannot shake off.

It pursued its road plans without much attention at all to broader planning considerations, although new roads have immense consequences for the shape of towns, the nature of employment and pressures on land use. The department "has developed in isolation from land-use planning, focused on road construction rather than overall transport planning, divorced from railway development or operation but has successfully promoted, built and justified substantial public investment in the trunk road network". Included in the department's remit were the motorways, which have

---

* In 2003 the Council for the Protection of Rural England became the Campaign to Protect Rural England, keeping the same initials (CPRE). This book uses the new name when referring to events after the change

turned most of rural England into a dormitory for workers in the big cities.

If the car as the destroyer of rolling country acres is relatively new, other concerns go back to the dawn of motoring. The car has always been seen as dangerous. It is pointed out that, relative to the number of vehicles in use, the car is less dangerous today than it was in the 1920s. The death toll, at around 3,500 a year for the UK, is broadly the same – on the face of it, a remarkable achievement with present traffic volumes – but it is nothing to shout about. Many of these are needless deaths caused by driver errors like speeding, misjudged overtaking or falling asleep at the wheel. To stay silent about these deaths is to say that there is an acceptable level of fatalities in exchange for the convenience of the car.

Our response as a society to traffic deaths suggests that we do see them in that light. Rail crashes generate enormous concern and extensive inquiries, yet the same level of deaths on the road, *every day*, goes unremarked. Punishments handed out in courts to offending motorists are often lenient, leading relatives of the dead to wail "Is that all his life was worth?" Until 1991, a century after the emergence of the car, there was not in English law an offence of causing death by dangerous driving. This left an unsatisfactory gap between the offences of reckless driving and manslaughter, so that drivers were commonly prosecuted on a lower level of charge than the circumstances required.

Society's implicit bargain with motor traffic is well illustrated by the case of lorry driver Graham Jagger, who was involved in a crash with a minibus when five died. Magistrates at Hinckley (Leicestershire) heard that although Jagger had a sleeping disorder that caused drowsiness, he had been at the wheel for 13 hours. He was fined £2,500 and banned for driving for two years.

Even more leniently dealt with was Andrew Little-john, whose inattention at the wheel caused two deaths when his articulated lorry crossed the central reservation on the M5 and hit oncoming vehicles. He pleaded guilty to driving without due care and atten-tion, and walked away from Taunton magistrates court with a £170 fine plus £59 costs and six penalty points on his driving licence.

Security guard Ian Barton died when he was struck by a drink-driver, who fled the scene. Luciane Martel-lete later called an ambulance but did not give her name. Weston-super-Mare magistrates fined the 31-year-old chef £150 and temporarily banned her from driving. The Campaign Against Drink Driving said: "Only when JPs take these cases seriously will drink-drivers get the message."

As a society we face two ways on motoring safety. We condone cutting corners but have little tolerance when others do the same and come unstuck. Many people criticised the five-year sentence received by builder Gary Hart as too lenient. Hart fell asleep at the wheel of his Land Rover and caused a rail crash at Selby in February 2001 in which 10 died. He had spent hours through the night talking on the phone to a woman he met on the internet, and then set out on a 150-mile (240km) drive to work. Hart's vehicle ran off the road on to the West Coast mainline, where it was hit by an express train. With an estimated closing speed of 147mph (237kph), this train was forced into the path of a goods train. Mr Justice Mackay, sentenc-ing Hart at Leeds Crown Court, described Selby as "perhaps the worst driving-related incident" in recent years. He noted that Hart was "shocked and angry" at his conviction.

A speeding car driver who hit a pregnant woman causing the death of her unborn son was sentenced to four years, and a drink driver who drove at 90mph

(145kph) through a town received 4 1/2 years: he killed three people when his car was in a head-on collision. In the second case Mike Jobbing of the Campaign Against Drink Driving said: "He will only end up serving 2 1/4 years, which means each life he took is being valued by the courts at less than a year."

A driver reversed his Range Rover into a girl of four in a bicycle trailer during a road rage incident. The girl suffered head injuries and lost five teeth. He was jailed for just two years.

Stiffer sentences were handed out to John McKinney at Lincoln and Ian Carr at Newcastle upon Tyne. McKinney, in another road rage incident, was jailed for life for deliberately running down teacher Gordon Springall, who survived. Carr received 9 1/2 years for killing six-year-old Rebecca Sawyer on New Year's Eve when he jumped a red light in a stolen vehicle and hit the car she was travelling in.

Minibuses are an illustration of society's safety compromise with motor vehicles. With seats jammed in right to the back, the rear passengers lack the barrier of a boot or stowage space as in a saloon car. Vulnerable to rear-end collisions, minibuses are unsuitable for long journeys at high speed, yet they are a common sight on motorways. What minibuses have in their favour are cheapness and ease of operation – the driver does not need a special licence.

A minibus ran into a vehicle parked on the hard shoulder of the London-Birmingham motorway, killing the driver and 12 schoolchildren. The driver, who was the children's teacher, appears to have fallen asleep at the wheel. It emerged that she had been teaching all day, had then driven the children from Birmingham to London for a concert, and was driving them back when the crash occurred.

It is astonishing that anyone should think it reasonable to do a full day's work and then attempt a return trip of more than 200 miles (320km). Yet this incident was probably unusual only in that it ended with a crash. The driver's misjudgement in making the trip was hardly remarked on publicly. Was this out of understandable sympathy for the dead woman or an illustration that society shares her assumption that there was nothing wrong in that course of action?

Despite years of publicity about the risk of "concertina collisions", two people died and more than 100 were injured in a pileup involving 100 vehicles on the M40 motorway north of High Wycombe. Cars were still colliding when police arrived. With wearisome inevitability the police reported that drivers had been going too fast in foggy conditions.

Road users don't have a monopoly of skimping on safety. The Connex train operating company, faced with a staff shortage, was aggrieved that many drivers did not want to work on their rest days. Talks with ASLEF, the drivers' union, turned on whether rest day working would be required or voluntary. In this widely noticed case, there was little or no thought expressed that rest days are there for a purpose and that to work them is a safety issue. This was just weeks after the horrendous rail crash near Paddington station, London, in October 1999, that claimed 31 lives.

The corruption of the best is the worst, and the casual climate towards road safety affects even the professionals. Lorry driver Paul Browning was found to have sent a text message on his mobile phone while driving. He struck and killed a young man who was standing beside a vehicle in a layby. Judge Daniel Worsley, sentencing Browning at Southend Crown Court, said: "In many ways it is difficult to imagine a more blatant act of such cold-blooded disregard for safety on the roads."

Browning admitted causing death by dangerous driving, but denied he was sending a text message at the time of the crash. The judge heard evidence despite the guilty plea so that he could ascertain whether the prosecution's claims about text messaging were true. He said "a stern deterrent sentence" was necessary, and sent Browning to prison for five years. Browning was said to be remorseful, and in one respect he, too, was a victim. His action was different in degree, not kind, from thousands of others every day. He was a victim of the casual safety culture that permeates Britain's roads.

Mobile phones are only one among a range of facilities to tempt drivers away from what should be their sole activity in a moving car: driving. Only one, but probably the most potentially lethal. A landmark study published in 2002 found that using a mobile phone at the wheel is more dangerous than drink driving.

The study, by the respected Transport Research Laboratory (TRL), found that typical reaction times of drivers using hand-held mobile phones were 30 per cent slower than those of alcohol-impaired drivers. Hands-free phones also increased reaction times. The UK blood alcohol limit is 80mg/100ml. At 70mph (113kph) drivers using mobile phones took almost half as long again to stop as drivers without distractions. Compared with a normal stopping distance of 102ft (31m) at that speed, alcohol-impaired drivers stopped in 115ft (35m) – but drivers using hand-held phones needed 148ft (45m) and those on hands-free phones 128ft (39m).

The survey was commissioned by insurer Direct Line. Spokesman Dominic Burch explained: "We chose to quantify the risk involved by comparing driving performance while using a mobile phone to driving while over the legal alcohol limit. Drink driving is clearly an established danger in the eyes of drivers. Eventually we would like to see the use of mobile phones when driving, both hands-held and hands-free, become as socially unacceptable as drink driving."

It would be a start if driving a public service vehicle while using a mobile phone became socially unacceptable. It is an all too common experience to see bus and coach drivers chatting on a mobile while the lives of many passengers depend on their concentration.

Soon after the TRL's shock survey, the government announced that it planned to ban the use of handheld mobile phones when driving – leaving drivers able to use hands-free phones. The ban came into force in December 2003, but its impact was reduced by the small fixed penalty (£30) and the failure, at least so far, to make infringement an endorsable offence.

From a time when the only communication device was to stop at the next public telephone box we have reached the point where drivers can make their cars their offices. The tone of the media when reporting new motoring gadgetry is invariably breathless, as with this typical example: "Ford's 24.7 concept cars – a saloon, estate and pick-up – are suitably big, boxy and versatile. Yet their interiors posit a brave new world of internet access and having your e-mail read to you by your dashboard. Don't fret: you talk face-to-facia to switch on wipers and lights and, inevitably, log on to any internet chat room you fancy." The "wholly interactive car" was said to be "a favourite notion" of Ford's vice-president of design, J. Mays.

Faced with the technology people can hardly be blamed for using it. But it would take a cock-eyed optimist to believe that drivers will use mobile phones, listen to their emails and take part in internet chat only when the car is snugly parked in a layby.

Convenience features in cars may threaten the safety not only of those outside the vehicle – as more efficient brakes persuade drivers to storm up to T-junctions ever faster, for example – but even of the car occupants. Thus the monster devours its own. Five-year-old Sarah Henderson died in the most harrowing way imaginable when a Mercedes 230 estate car rolled into the River Thames at Shepperton. Her grandfather had started the car and then returned to the house to fetch his glasses. Despite desperate rescue efforts by Sarah's father as the car moved forward, she could not be freed from the back seat where she was strapped in and drowned in the river.

She died because of three elements in the design of the luxury vehicle – two of which are purely convenience features. The parking brake on the Mercedes was foot-operated, making it impossible, according to a police accident investigations officer, to apply the brake from the passenger side while the car was moving. An automatic choke was installed which, the investigator explained, would operate in cold weather tending to move the vehicle forward.

Even if Sarah had freed herself from the seat belt she still would not have got out. Child safety locks meant the back doors could be opened only from the outside. To assess the true safety value of childproof locks, we need to consider how many children actually fell out of moving cars before locks were installed. The tragedy is that little Sarah would not have died in a car from before the era of special features – a car with a handbrake, a manual choke and back doors that could be opened from inside.

The motoring lobby hails it as an achievement that roads are not becoming more dangerous despite the huge growth in car use. Yet a key reason for the constant level of fatalities despite the growth of traffic is that Britain's roads and streets are virtual no-go areas for anything except motor vehicles. There is no finer sight than the traffic stream brought to a halt by a herd of cows being driven along the road! It is a reminder that the highway is for everyone. However, pedestrians and even cyclists are scared of using many cross-country roads, while in the towns and cities children cannot safely play in the streets by their homes. The absence of other types of road user creates another self-reinforcing spiral: the fewer the other road users the more motorists drive as if there is no-one else, while the more they drive as if there is no-one else even fewer are others who dare to use the roads. So cars rocket round blind corners on the assumption of nothing except another car on the other side, or storm along country roads as if nothing ever emerges through field gates.

As a response to the growing threat to cyclists on the roads, dedicated cycleways are created in the towns and cities. But these remain pitifully few in number. They are also a mixed blessing: the more such cycleways, the more motorists will feel that cyclists have no right on the roads. No doubt a ban already exists as a gleam in some planner's eye. Probably few cyclists would accept being isolated from the road even where an equivalent track exists.

Cycleways can be bad news for pedestrians. Often the tracks are created simply by painting a white line along the pavement and declaring one side for walkers and the other side for bikes. This encourages riding on pavements whether designated or not. The niceties of the law, which says you can ride along these pavements but it is an offence to ride on pavements not so designated, are understandably missed by many young cyclists. They ride along crowded city pavements probably unaware that they are breaking the law. In any case, they have been doing it since the beginning. Their parents strictly forbade them to cycle on the dangerous roads. Pavement riding by cyclists is one of the biggest complaints of pedestrians, but it is understandable why cyclists do it. Ultimately, both groups are victims of the madcap roads.

"Pavement rage" is surely a syndrome waiting to happen. Pedestrians are threatened by tearaway cyclists, and their way is often blocked by cars that colonise the walkways. Thoughtless pavement parking has become endemic.

It is hard to see who are not victims of Britain's roads. Numerous incidents of road rage testify to the intolerable pressures faced by drivers. A motorist in Denholme, near Bradford, was angry because all the parking spaces near his house were taken. He was reported to have used his Range Rover as a battering ram to create a space, causing £150,000-worth of damage.

The growth of motor traffic has swept aside every other category of road user, whether walker, cyclist, horse rider or cow herder, in terms of their comfort and convenience even when it is not threatening their safety. At least, we may think, car (and lorry) drivers are safer in their vehicles than they have ever been. The motor industry extols every sort of safety feature, and no doubt has some more up its sleeve to be introduced over time. For the drivers this level of security may be an illusion. More effective brakes don't lead to more effective braking: instead, as any pedestrian or cyclist will testify, they allow drivers to approach corners and junctions faster than they did before – returning the risk of an accident to its former level. In other words, drivers adapt their behaviour to circumstances, maintaining a constant level of risk that each individual finds acceptable. Thus safety benefits become adopted as performance benefits, as Robert Davis indicates in *Death on the Streets**. "Interventions for 'road safety' tend to redistribute danger and accidents, rather than eliminate them," he says.

This idea of risk compensation seems bleak, but its value is to suggest that safety benefits as such will not solve the problem.

***

* (Leading Edge Press and Publishing, 1993)

Dr Gerda Reith, a lecturer in sociology at Glasgow University, pointed out that human beings have a dual way of looking at risk. She said: "If you want something quite badly and there's not much chance you're going to get it, you tend to think that the probability of getting it is higher than it really is [ie, winning the National Lottery]. But if there's something negative that could happen to you, then you tend to think that it won't happen." On just such a basis do millions of us drive every day.

We should have fewer road deaths if cars were not able to go so fast and accelerate so quickly. Those who are quick to make the social case for the car would be hard pressed to say why we must be able to travel at 120mph (190kph) or accelerate from 0 to 60 in 10 seconds.

If driving more slowly is the answer, devices to help business users detect speed cameras spread the opposite message of carrying on as before. Morpheous Ltd, of Rochester, announced "Fatalities from road accidents have fallen by up to 50 per cent in areas where speed cameras have been fitted" and "Speed cameras are set to triple in number over the next few years". The logic of such information is surely to co-operate with the cameras – but what was being offered was a "speed camera warning device" called Geodesy, linked to a satellite-based global positioning system which "pinpoints the location of every known speed camera in England, Scotland and Wales and warns you as you are approaching one". It was stressed – twice – that such a device is legal.

In the dawn of motoring the car was hailed as the paragon of cleanness that would clear the streets of horse droppings. So it has. Yet we would not think much of a doctor who cured a skin ailment while failing to deal with kidney disease. Streets are clean of horse droppings, and much worse pollution fills the air.

Pollutants produced by motor vehicles include nitrogen oxides, particulates, benzene, hydrocarbons, carbon monoxide and carbon dioxide. Except for the last, these threaten health by raising the risk of respiratory ailments, coronary problems and cancer. Catalytic converters reduce emissions of hydrocarbons and carbon monoxide but increase the output of carbon dioxide, the main greenhouse gas behind global warming. Motor traffic is a major source of carbon dioxide (CO_2) produced by the burning of fossil fuels. An excess of CO_2 is produced coming on top of the natural processes of respiration and photosynthesis.

Diesel engines are increasingly popular for reasons that are nothing to do with the environment: they are cheaper to run and their performance has been vastly improved. Unfortunately, diesels are at once greener and less healthy, putting the ecologically minded motorist in a quandary. Diesel produces less carbon dioxide than a petrol engine, but more nitrogen oxide and particulates. A badly maintained diesel engine is much "dirtier" than a badly maintained petrol engine.

Professor Roy Harrison of Birmingham University said US research extrapolated to Britain suggested that particulates caused about 4,000 lung cancer deaths a year – about one-tenth of the total. The provisional figures indicated that mortality rates increased six per cent for every additional 10 microgrammes of particles per cubic metre of air.

The petrol-driven internal combustion engine, frequently written off over the past 50 years, has shown a tenacious hold on survival. Manufacturers are often accused of not trying hard enough to produce cleaner alternatives, but they say that we the public don't want them.

Among the alternative power sources that have been used at least in prototype cars:

Electricity. This power source has been around almost as long as cars have, and is surrounded by many myths. Modern electric cars are not milk floats: they can easily reach the legal speed limit, but the weight of batteries and the relatively short distance the vehicle can travel between charges remain problems. Electric vehicles are well suited to the stop-start conditions of urban motoring, where petrol-powered cars produce their worst pollution. However, electricity also has environmental downsides, whether it is generated from fossil fuels or by nuclear fission.

Electricity + petrol. An ingenious technology where the power source used depends on the road circumstances. Disliked by some as a halfway house and liked by others as getting the best of both worlds. The Toyota Prius is a firm favourite with greens.

LPG (liquefied petroleum gas). A practical proposition for today's motorists concerned to reduce polluting emissions. More than four million cars worldwide are reported to be running on LPG. Petrol and diesel vehicles can be converted relatively cheaply.

Natural gas. Also attractive for lower emissions, but huge costs will be involved in setting up the infrastructure if this fuel is to be viable for private motorists rather than buses, which operate in fixed areas.

Hydrogen fuel cell. The ultimate clean power source – the only byproduct is water vapour. Electricity to drive the vehicle is generated from hydrogen and oxygen passing over electrodes. Storage of hydrogen at the correct temperature has proved difficult and, for safety, potential leaks must be constantly monitored and avoided. Critics say so much energy is needed to produce the hydrogen that the technology is not green anyway. Furthermore, the original source of energy might be nuclear, the greens' ultimate bete noire.

General Motors demonstrated a prototype hydrogen-powered car called Hy-wire, with the motive unit producing 94 kilowatts of power (equivalent to 126bhp). Its performance characteristics were stated as: top speed 100mph (160kph); 0-60mph (97kph), 16 seconds; fuel consumption, equivalent to 16-35mpg (5.7-12.4km per litre). Russell Bray of the Mail on Sunday reported on the unusual ride: "Frankly, the silence when cruising is eerie. Pedestrians wouldn't hear you coming ... just the gentle hiss of steam coming from the exhaust pipe."

Biofuels. The ultimate recycling proposition. All sorts of vegetable oils can be converted into fuel for diesel engines, so the fish-and-chip oil doesn't have to be thrown away. The people of Llannelli, Wales, put supermarket cooking oil to good use, but were stopped by the police because excise duty on petrol was being lost.

Biodiesel is produced by adding methanol to vegetable oil. This removes the glycerin, leaving a fuel that works the engine like diesel from petroleum.

The potential of biodiesel has grown with the spreading popularity of diesel engines. The inventor of diesel, Rudolph Diesel, expected his engine to run like this. In 1900 he demonstrated the engine running on converted peanut oil. John Vidal wrote in the Guardian: "Diesel was motivated by a humanitarian vision. He thought that his highly efficient engine, which was adaptable in size and could use various fuels, would allow threatened independent craftsmen and artisans to take on the large industries which virtually monopolised the dominant power source of the time – the expensive, fuel-wasting steam engine."

While alternatives to petrol were available at the dawn of motoring, the diesel engine was held back for many years by its inferior performance and greater noise. Modern diesel engines are unrecognisable in both regards, so for the typical motorist these problems have been solved.

From the fate of the planet to the fate of the family, the chickens have come home to roost. Most parents wonder whether the rise in childhood asthma and the increase in motor vehicles are connected. Few non-parents, too, would wish to be part of a society that knowingly gives its children asthma. But the link between asthma and pollution is unproved – indeed, strongly disputed – so we feel free to avoid the precautionary principle and carry on as before.

In Britain, a prime cause of environmental pollution are juggernaut lorries carrying goods that could far more cleanly be carried by rail. The CPRE's *Where Motor-Car Is Master*, makes clear that rail freight had been declining for decades before juggernauts came along. Now everyone (except hauliers) wants goods back on the railways, but the die was cast as far back as the Fifties. The huge public investment in building motorways, which started in that period, was a hidden subsidy for road haulage. The desirability of keeping freight on the railways was recognised, but British governments of the day did little about it: "In many other countries it was realised that the construction of large motorway systems brought a need to regulate road haulage operations in the wider interest; but in the UK the Ministry [of Transport] merely deplored the railway deficit and washed its hands of the fact that its own actions were increasing the railway's freight difficulties."

Juggernauts are the offspring of motorways, but they have become common on lesser roads and urban streets as they make deliveries to stores. One of the worst pollution problems caused by the use, or rather misuse, of motor vehicles is the system of "just in time" deliveries. It means that supermarkets no longer maintain large warehouse stocks, but receive deliveries daily of the items they need (including exotic fruit and vegetables air-freighted into the country – itself a big environmental issue). It also means fleets of lorries, many mainly empty, dashing around the country. These journeys would not be needed with conventional warehousing. Praised by business leaders and hailed as an extension of consumer choice, just-in-time is a case of business being unwilling to look beyond short-term profits to the wider social issues.

Belatedly, it has become part of the common wisdom that trains are less polluting per passenger or ton of goods carried than road vehicles. A great deal of effort and investment is going into reinstalling rail systems that were removed a generation ago. Trams were mainly shut down in the Fifties amid the postwar euphoria for a brave new world. With less justification – because road traffic was already showing its soar-away rise – the railway system was savagely cut back in the Beeching era. Now, for example, Manchester and Croydon (South London) have trams again, while the main railway line between High Wycombe and Banbury (a route from London to Birmingham) has been double-tracked, or rather re-double-tracked, after having previously been taken down to single.

To restore a railway that has been dismantled is a much tougher proposition than dualising the line because parts of the trackbed may have been built upon or the infrastructure of bridges, tunnels, embankments and cuttings may have fallen into disrepair. However, there is an ambitious plan to reopen the Great Central railway for goods working. This was the last of the main lines into London, and when it was closed in the Sixties there were wellwishers on platforms who had seen it open six decades earlier.

When Dorothy Wordsworth rented a cottage in Grasmere in the Lake District she was worried that her poet brother William would be disturbed by the passage of the carrier's cart twice a day. Modern writers would think themselves fortunate with one hundred times that traffic flow.

In The Missing Three-Quarter, Sherlock Holmes describes a fruitless search in the Cambridge area for the vanished man: "Chesterton, Histon, Waterbeach, and Oakington have each been explored, and have each proved disappointing. The daily appearance of a brougham and pair could hardly have been overlooked in such Sleepy Hollows" (from *The Return of Sherlock Holmes*, 1904). See them now!

We have become desensitised to noise so that we barely notice the river of traffic flowing past our doors in the cities or the motorbike scramblers beating up bridleways in the country. Often it is the most attractive streets that suffer the most: the avenues in towns laid out before the motor age and picture postcard villages where vehicles force their way through habitations set down in medieval times. There is no respite from traffic noise over vast areas of the countryside. Motorways can be heard from two miles (3.2km) away, or more. (See the Council for the Protection of Rural England's "tranquil areas" typology in Chapter Three.)

Noise nuisance is compounded by a culture of heedlessness among drivers. The arrogant motorist of yesteryear has become Everyman in his lack of awareness of those around him. A single car or motorbike with a faulty exhaust (or one that has been intentionally altered) sends an in-yer-face message that is heard in hundreds of homes. People who would not think of singing and dancing in the street at three in the morning are happy to stay chatting around the car with the engine running. It is seen as normal to treat the car to a prolonged (and unnecessary) "warm-up" at 6.30am, a time well calculated to wake up neighbours in front bedrooms. Doorbells could be removed for all the use that taxi drivers make of them: the only way to announce one's arrival is to sound the horn, whether it is four in the afternoon or four in the morning. The story of the car is about the atomisation of society. For Philip E. Slater, in *The Pursuit of Loneliness* (1970)*, a private means of transport is one of the ways in which Americans "attempt to minimize, circumvent, or deny the interdependence upon which all human societies are based". He wrote: "An enormous technology seems to have set itself the task of making it unnecessary for one human being ever to ask anything of another in the course of going about his daily business." Slater's other examples are a private house, a private garden, a private laundry, self-service stores and do-it-yourself skills. More than three decades after Slater published his memorable counter-cultural text, he could as well be writing about Britain and much if not all of the Western world: we are all Americans now.

Because of this desire for avoidance "we less and less often meet our fellow man to share and exchange, and more and more often encounter him as an impediment or a nuisance: making the highway crowded when we are rushing somewhere ... taking the last parking place ... Because we have cut off so much communication with each other we keep bumping into each other, and thus a higher and higher percentage of our interpersonal contacts are abrasive." So is road rage born of the culture of isolation.

In Coventry Cathedral in 1996, a service to celebrate the centenary of the motor car proved too much for campaigner Angel Quercus. In the city of Lady Godiva and supported by members of Friends of the Earth and Roadpeace, she appeared naked in the cathedral shouting, "This is in memory of my mother

* (Beacon Press, Boston)

and thousands of others who have died." The service acknowledged the downside of the car before celebrating the motor industry as "the lifeblood of the Midlands". As the highlight of the service an 1897 Daimler and a new electric Peugeot 106 were driven down the cathedral aisle.

If the 20th century was the century of the car, it remains to be seen whether the 21st century will be any different. So far the signs are unpromising. In December 2002 the transport secretary, Alastair Darling, admitted that road congestion would not be five per cent less in 2010 as called for in the government's 10-year transport plan. On the contrary – in a message of deep gloom for those already in despair at the country's strangulating roads – congestion was expected to *rise* by 11 to 20 per cent. On motorways and main trunk roads the increase would be one to 15 per cent, and in large towns and cities it would be nine to 20 per cent. We are addicts who know about the amenity, safety, pollution and noise problems, but we are willing to lay all aside for the next fix of sheer convenience.

TWO
A WORLD THAT MIGHT
HAVE BEEN

IF the policymakers of 1910 had been able to see the
long-term effects of the car, it is unimaginable that
they would have acted as they did. Or rather as they
failed to act to balance car use with broader social
needs. It is unimaginable, for instance, that the
prospect of cars being driven into Britain's towns and
cities each with a single occupant would have been tol-
erated. Traffic growth has been unrestrained and until
recently the policy was to build more roads to accommodate it. Even in 2002 and again in 2003 the government was announcing a programme of major road-
building, although mainly so-called improvements to
existing motorways and trunk roads.

New Labour's brave plans on taking office in 1997
about restraining car use died with the motorists' fuel
tax revolt of 2000 – the only time between the Blair
government's coming to power in 1997 and the Hutton
inquiry of 2003 that Labour lost its electoral lead over
the Conservatives. Matters of war, pensions, health
and public transport might be shrugged off by battered
voters, but cars never!

In 1910, policymakers could not know that the car,
still little more than a hobby for the rich, would
become the beloved monster of today. At first sight, the
policymakers of 1950 have more to answer for. This
was at the edge of the period when car use in Britain
leaped upwards: the policy response not only failed to
foresee the dangers but also stimulated traffic growth

by planning super-fast inter-urban motorways. However, to curb traffic would have been politically impossible by then. It would have denied mobility to blue-collar people just when they were able to afford it. The only time that the motorisation of the world might have taken a different road was at the beginning.

Traffic has grown under a laisser faire paradigm where roads are free for all and anyone who can afford a vehicle can have one. It needn't have been that way. The ancient right to use the highway looks very different when towns and cities are choking with traffic and children, asthmatic or not, are driven from the streets where they used to play.

The alternative social benefit paradigm – stillborn in 1910 – sees road space as a scarce resource to be rationed for the general good. It also also recognises that vehicles can be dangerous as well as useful – another sufficient reason for the state to act. Few people have difficulty with the *principle* of restricting use of scarce resources or dangerous substances, although they may bitterly dispute where that principle is applied (particularly with cars). Radio frequencies, for example, are allocated by the authorities to protect emergency communications and to avoid a babel of overlapping broadcasts. Heroin cannot be brought across the counter because the state recognises a duty to discourage an individual's self-destruction.

Another group of everyday products are useful and dangerous at the same time. Tobacco, the trigger for a range of conditions from cancer to hypertension, is pleasant to smoke. The humble aspirin can cure our headaches, but may cause gastro-intestinal bleeding. If their downsides had been realised at the outset, tobacco would probably be banned and aspirin available only on prescription. If our Edwardian forebears had been able to see the future, the ubiquitous car would have been similarly restricted.

We can imagine the effects of the social benefit paradigm if it had prevailed in 1910:

Cars stayed a luxury, brought about by taxation, making the driving test more difficult (incredibly, there was no compulsory driving test in Britain as late as the 1930s) – and simply not making up the roads. In reality, the extensive programme of tarring roads carried out in the 1920s encouraged more traffic as the road-building programme did later on.

Cars became less attractive when manufacturers cooperated with the government in limiting performance. Engines were made to produce a top speed of 55mph (88kph) – plenty enough for personal mobility but not enough to encourage speed merchants, whose needs were catered for in off-road leisure circuits. Private alteration of a car to increase its performance became a criminal offence and largely ceased to exist. Like cock fighting, also illegal, it happened but in secret and on a small scale.

Limiting the top speed of cars gave a fillip to railway travel. With trains able to travel at more than twice the speed of cars, it seemed pointless to use the car for long-distance journeys. Buying a car became a discretionary purchase with many who could afford it choosing not to. Ordinary people did not resent being car-less anymore than they resented not being able to dine at the Ritz Hotel: what mattered was alternative transport arrangements. The railways flourished, both for long-distance and commuter journeys. Towns and cities stayed compact, and expansion tended to follow the railway lines, so no-one was very far from a station.

The railways enjoyed a benign circle of increasing investment and traffic growth. Much of the investment came from the government, which put the railways at the centre of national transport strategy. The attraction of trains was increased by the switch to diesel and electric. Britain was among the world's leaders, and steam engines were largely phased out in the 1930s (a generation before it actually happened).

The railways continued to be the main carriers of goods traffic. Roads were unsuitable for long-distance haulage, so rail and road maintained their 19th century partnership with lorries taking the freight onwards for local delivery. Of course, improvements were made to reduce transshipment costs and delay. These included packaging goods in containers and ingenious "road-railers" that ran on both track and road.

Opinion surveys found little dissatisfaction among the car-less, who in the interwar period were helped by the improvement of the railways, the spread of bus services and innovative council schemes to collect people from their homes (of the sort that actually were not tried until half a century later by which time the genie of universal car ownership was out of the bottle).

Buoyant demand produced a flourishing car hire sector. Many people declared that it was pointless to buy a car when one could be so easily borrowed. Nobody was refused because of his or her insurance record: the government was the insurer for hire cars, and its client base was so large that it could easily accommodate a few bad drivers.

The expansion of the railways, together with shipbuilding, continued the demand for steel and engineering components, but these industries did not grow in the way they would have if cars had gone into mass production. As a result thousands were spared the tyranny of the low-paid assembly line, finding employment instead in a range of high-value craft industries and social work activities. Car factories were small scale, with much work done by hand. The conveyor belt – tried by Henry Ford in the United States, but with limited success – was a rarity.

Although the motorisation of the world generally proceeded in a controlled and considered way, there were renegade countries. France was famous for its let-'em-rip approach to cars, and Paris was noted for its traffic jams. Cars were much cheaper in that country, which sometimes made visitors angry – until they thought about the traffic jams and the running costs.

Could it have happened that way? There is nothing unimaginable   about the scenario just described. A really radical policy would be to restrict car use to the groups that need it most, the teens and twenties, and the elderly – in other words, reversing the present pattern where the young and the old have the least access to cars. Society could consider an arrangement by which people may own cars up to age 30 – they have the most busy social lives and enjoy the thrill of movement most – and again from age 60 – when mobility by other means may be difficult. People between 30 and 59 are the group best able to do without cars by using buses, trains, taxis or bicycles.

The social benefit paradigm, many will say, could never have prevailed because economics dictated otherwise. And yet in the interwar period it was generally believed that "road and rail transport were by nature complementary", according to Peter Thorold's *The Motoring Age* (Profile Books, 2003), for goods and for commuters. Perhaps a small shift in attitude by government would have kept them that way.

It is surely dangerous to argue that the way things happened is the only way they *could have* happened. For example, it is hard to see that the Protestant Reformation was *bound to happen* in some countries of 16th century Europe and not others, while in yet other countries it was done and then undone; but that is how events worked out, forever changing the history and character of Europe.

The laisser faire paradigm has determined the history of motoring to date. A paradigm is about people's understanding and attitudes. Under another paradigm, the outcome would have been different because the economic forces would have been redirected.

Present attempts to manage car usage, like the graduated tax on carbon dioxide emissions, are welcome but may be far too late in the day. Certainly they will fail unless motorists experience a dramatic change of attitude – a conversion on the North Circular Road. There is a smack of desperation about traffic calming schemes, pedestrianised town centres and roundabouts in the middle of the countryside. They treat the symptoms but not the cause of the illness, which is too much traffic.

There is no government campaign adapting the Second World War slogan: is your (car) journey really necessary? Nor – to draw from the imaginary scenario – is there the remotest attempt to tackle the problem at the supply end: the cars themselves, and the way they are aggressively advertised. Manufacturers have a heavy responsibility for creating much of the danger of motoring but behind the manufacturers are we, the public, ever eager for the next drop of performance. If performance was reduced it would be a win all round.

A car with a top speed of 60mph (97kph) would do all the jobs that drivers claim to need it for; it would be safer, use less fuel and, being unable to compete on speed, boost the attraction of railways.

Meanwhile, a Dutch experiment suggested that traffic lights and lane markings actually make roads less safe. The fatality rate at dangerous junctions dropped to zero when traffic lights were removed. The reason for the improvement was that drivers had to keep eye contact with other vehicles, cyclists and pedestrians instead of allowing the signals to dictate their driving behaviour. They slowed down to less than 20 mph (32 kph), when a child is five times more likely to survive than one hit at more than 30 mph (48 kph).

The same reverse psychology was used by Wiltshire County Council, which removed the centre white lines on sections of five main roads. All were in or near towns. A council official said the lack of central guidelines created "a measure of uncertainty" and made drivers more careful.

According to the Commission for Integrated Transport, Britain has the most congested roads and worst commuting times in Europe (and, according to government projections, it is expected to get worse). Almost a quarter of main inter-urban roads suffered delays of an hour or more compared with nine per cent in Italy, eight per cent in Germany and four per cent in France. British roads were used more intensively than in any other European Union country except Spain.

The commission, which was advising the government, said roads and railways had been "starved of investment" for half a century and public spending on infrastructure still lagged behind that in most EU states.

Although there is almost one car for every two adults in Britain, vehicle ownership clearly has not reached saturation point. Perhaps, like infinity, saturation will never be reached. In the United States, there are more cars than licensed drivers.

In Britain, the number of cars is predicted to increase by a third over a decade. By 2016, according to the government's Highways Agency, traffic will be between 36 per cent and 57 per cent higher than in 1996. The agency found that motorways and trunk routes made up four per cent of the country's roads but carried 67 per cent of road-borne freight traffic. Most of these cargoes would be travelling long distance, underlining the opportunities for rail transit.

Commercial traffic, however, has switched so decisively to road that it needs the faith that moves mountains to foresee another distribution pattern. In the meantime, a hillock was shifted in November 2003 with an announcement about parcels, long driven off the railways in significant numbers. English Welsh & Scottish Railway was to establish a network of parcel services from Walsall in northern England to Mossend, Aberdeen and Inverness in Scotland with trains travelling at up to 110mph (180kph). The £1m project, which was mainly funded by the Scottish Executive, was said to enable nearly one million lorry miles (1.6m km) to be removed from Scotland's roads each year. EWS was eyeing a London to Scotland parcels service.

Twenty-eight academics headed by Professor Phil Goodwin of University College, London wrote an open letter to the British government urging more action to manage worsening traffic conditions. Professor Goodwin said: "On current trends we expect progressive, steady deterioration in traffic conditions and congestion. There isn't any possible way of building enough road capacity to outpace growth in traffic."

In London, the school run was exposed as a major contributor to congestion in figures compiled by Trafficmaster for the Evening Standard. During half-term journey times were reduced by up to 50 per cent.

The "school run" proves to be an understatement as parents use their cars to carry children to an ever-widening range of activities. A survey for car repairers Autoglass found that London mothers typically make 28 trips a week ferrying children – with a high price tag for themselves and other road users. In the stress of trying to get somewhere on time, mothers were even prepared to put their own children at risk. One in five had been involved in an accident on these trips, more than one in three sometimes forgot to belt up their children and a similar number admitting cutting up other vehicles. More than half admitted jumping traffic lights.

One of the world's most ambitious attempts at traffic control was launched in London in February 2003, covering a central zone of eight square miles (21 sq km). Mayor Ken Livingstone, it was widely believed, had grasped a nettle that other politicians avoided. Drivers entering the congestion charge zone had to pre-pay £5 a day, with exceptions for essential users and reductions for zone residents. Those who entered the zone without having paid were sent penalty notices.

The computerised charging system – based on cameras reading number plates – suffered many teething troubles, with frequent complaints of cars being recorded when they were nowhere near London. However, by the autumn the mayor was buoyant about the scheme. The official report, *Congestion Charging: Six Months On*, said motor vehicles entering the zone were down by 16 per cent and congestion was at its lowest since the mid-1980s. Traffic delays within the zone were down by 30 per cent. Penalty charge notices were being issued at an average of 106,200 a month, but "representations" about the penalties (by drivers who for one reason or another thought they should not pay) had fallen to 16 per cent.

According to the report, 50,000 fewer cars per day were entering the charge zone, but only 4,000 fewer people – suggesting a shift to the use of public transport.

The report tackled head-on two of the main criticisms of the congestion charge: that it keeps customers away from city centre shops and that it merely adds to traffic outside the charge zone. *Congestion Charging: Six Months On* claimed no significant traffic displacement to local roads around the zone had been observed. It argued that retailers were suffering a recession in the first part of 2003 and the congestion charge was responsible for only five to seven per cent of the loss of potential customers (ie, people in the charging zone).

A substantial minority of Londoners – 30 per cent – continued to oppose the scheme, and the report acknowledged that revenue had been less than expected. The scheme's effectiveness will continue to be disputed. As a first step in reclaiming the streets for people, however, it has brought hope in the darkness.

Among policymakers an alternative to the laisser faire paradigm is struggling to emerge, although some have yet to catch up with the landmark Royal Commission on Environmental Pollution, which in 1994 published a wide-ranging blueprint of 100 proposals to shake the country's obsession with the car. Of lasting significance is the commission's detailed analysis, showing how the car came from almost nowhere after the Second World War to overwhelm other modes of travel. It called for a reduction in the roads programme with the then-novel observation that new roads actually increase traffic.

The former Conservative government started down the green trail by rejecting some road schemes, particularly Oxleas Wood in London, and the present Labour government has taken a cautiously tougher line on car use. The extreme sensitivity of the subject, however, is shown by the government's quick abandonment of the plan to raise petrol prices after a mass protest by motorists.

There is little sign of a shift of attitudes where it matters most, by us the public. Drivers may agree in general that traffic growth must be curbed, but bitterly oppose the particular ways of bringing that about, like congestion charges (a form of road pricing), emission taxes, dearer petrol – or giving up the car.

The issue of car ownership is bedevilled by an all-or-nothing approach. Some greens unwisely give the impression that the only virtuous motorist is the ex-motorist, but this approach helps the diehard driver. Every car owner can find at least one reason for keeping his car with a clear conscience.

A more productive approach is to think about a **ladder of substitution**. Here drivers voluntarily replace the car with bus, train or bicycle wherever it is practicable to do so. The more we give up, the higher on the ladder we find ourselves. The first rung is pretty painless: we take the bus instead of driving to the local Friends of the Earth meeting. The highest rung? Well, read on... The ladder of substitution is not a holier-than-thou, or rather higher-than-thou, exercise. Each individual and each family have different circumstances. We can all give up something in our use of the car. The ladder of substitution also rebuts the hoary excuses of motorists for carrying on regardless. They tend to defend themselves by citing an activity high up on the ladder and asking, "How could I do that without a car?" Probably they couldn't – but it is missing the point, which is to substitute another form of transport when we have the chance.

For those who try it the ladder seems pretty solid on its lower rungs, the middle rungs sway a bit while the higher rungs are positively vertiginous. Those who reach the top step onto the sunny plateau of green consciousness and probably find they don't need a car at all. For the rest, however, the car simply stays at home while the particular activity is undertaken.

The ladder of substitution appears on the next page.

In time, it might stop being socially acceptable to use the car for the activities represented at least by the lower rungs of the ladder, just as most people no longer see drink-driving as acceptable. It is through a process like this, rather than traffic management or penalty charges, that the world might, just might, return to motoring sanity. It remains a long shot. The best opportunity was lost in the dawn of motoring, and few drivers want to give up their wheels for a paradigm.

LADDER OF SUBSTITUTION

Replace the car with other forms of transport – train, bus, bicycle or taxi – for the following activities (the higher the number the harder the substitution)

20.	Go on a family camping holiday	
19.	Take bedridden parent on an outing	
18.	Go on first date with a sensational girl/boy	
17.	Buy DIY materials at B&Q	
16.	Make daily hospital visit to wife/husband	
15.	Make round of business calls	
14.	Lend car to children	
13.	Fetch children from a party	
12.	Be fetched after a country walk	
11.	Take a joyride	
10.	Commute to work through a car pool	
9.	Deliver children to an activity	
8.	Make an indirect business journey	
7.	Commute to work solo	
6.	Go to the supermarket	
5.	Do the school run	
4.	Visit a pub or restaurant	
3.	Make city-to-city business journey	
2.	Visit nearby corner shop	
1.	Attend local Friends of the Earth meeting	

THREE
AIRCRAFT AND THE
'1910 EFFECT'

JUST AS motor transport has conquered the land, so it is poised to conquer the air with many of the same problems in even greater form. Travellers queuing at overcrowded check-ins, or kept in a holding pattern over Britain's congested airports, may not think so but the expansion of aviation has only just begun. In car terms we are at 1910. Policymakers at that time could have no idea of the monster they were letting loose. With that precedent before us, we – policymakers, environmentalists, voters – can foresee the future of aviation, or rather, the future of aviation if we don't act.

The Department for Transport's July 2002 consultation document, *The Future Development of Air Transport in the United Kingdom*, was the forerunner of the white paper published in December 2003 setting out the government's plans for the future of commercial aviation (described in Chapter Four). The consultation document's headline prediction was a near trebling of demand for air travel by 2030. In response to this trend, the DfT signalled a huge expansion of airport capacity, with options including a third runway at Heathrow, up to three new runways at Stansted and a brand-new airport at Church Lawford, near Rugby.

To its critics the consultation document was a classic "predict and provide" exercise of the kind discredited for roads since at least the early 1990s (and with housing for more than half a century, since the Town and Country Planning Act 1947 put paid to building at will). The DfT insisted that the approach was not that of predict and provide, but for many people if it looked like a duck, walked like a duck and quacked like a duck it undoubtedly was a duck.

The number of air passengers across the country, if growth was unconstrained, was expected almost to treble by 2030, from 180 million to 500 million annually (with 300 million of these using airports in the South East). This could even be an underestimate, as the consultation document acknowledged. Growth scenarios have often been wrong, and this one was based on fare assumptions that looked shaky right at the start of the 28-year forecasting period. The figures assumed a one per cent per annum fall in fares in real terms, but fares have been continuing to fall at twice that rate.

Even more astonishing than the expected growth in passenger demand was that for air freight. The consultation document pointed out that air freight had doubled between 1969 and 1989, had doubled again in the following decade and was expected to rise even faster over the next 10 years. It was mainly high-value items – like tropical fruit and vegetables – and express parcels. If demand was unconstrained, it was predicted to rise from 2.1m tonnes in 1998 to 13.6m tonnes in 2030 – a more than sixfold increase (548 per cent). For anyone already troubled by night freight flights, the news got even worse: express parcels were expected to take a growing share of total freight demand. These, the consultation document explained, needed 24-hour airport operations for next-day deliveries. Already in 2000 at the main London airports (Heathrow, Gatwick, Stansted and Luton) there were a total of 13,000 air traffic movements (ATMs) between 10pm and 6am.

Ministers had clearly been persuaded by the economic case for aviation. It was "a great British success story". The industry provided more than 180,000 jobs in the UK, and indirectly supported three times that number of jobs. Foreign tourists, many of them carried by air, were worth £13bn a year - about one per cent of gross domestic product.

British Airways' chief economist, Dr Andrew Sentance, addressed the Confederation of British Industry's national conference in November 2002, and appealed to business leaders to get onside with airport expansion.

Quoting a report by Oxford Economic Forecasting, Sentance said good aviation links were vital for innovative high-technology and other high value-added industries, such as financial services. He declared: "The [aviation] industry cannot deliver these economic benefits unless it has access to the infrastructure needed to support its expansion."

Others are not persuaded by the aviation industry's favourite theme of economic benefits. The supposed need to keep the arteries of business open through airport expansion sits poorly with the fact that leisure is overwhelmingly the purpose of travel.* In the age of video-conferencing and the internet, the need for business travel is less. New airports and new runways create jobs, but the easier access to foreign goods and services also costs jobs in the home country. Ask fruit and vegetable farmers, or the hotel industry in British coastal resorts.

Aviation is part and parcel of globalisation, which has destroyed so many good manufacturing jobs in western countries replacing them with service sector "McJobs". Textiles and consumer electronics are among the UK casualties. The process - which damages workers in both the First and Third Worlds - is searingly described in Naomi Klein's *No Logo* (2000).

---

* See pages 65-66

Flying Into Trouble, published by the Aviation Environment Federation, cited a 1999 study by the government's Standing Advisory Committee on Trunk Road Assessment (SACTRA) and said new transport infrastructure does not necessarily lead to gains in economic performance. It helps with economic regeneration only if a range of other factors are also in place.

Quoting a Berkeley Hanover study in 2000, *Flying Into Trouble* said the economic effect of bringing aviation growth under control would not be a net loss of jobs: it would simply mean a different distribution of jobs around Britain. Money not spent on air travel would be spent on other goods and services, creating jobs in those sectors.

The much-vaunted tourism card was trumped by Tony Grayling and Simon Bishop in their study, *Sustainable Aviation 2030,* for the centre-left Institute for Public Policy Research: they pointed out that Britons spend more abroad than visitors do in Britain, representing a net flow of spending out of the country. Their conclusions were confirmed by figures from the Office of National Statistics, showing that in 2002 for every visit to the UK from overseas Britons made more than two visits abroad.

When transport secretary Alistair Darling said "doing nothing is not an option", he cemented the view that the government was ready to accommodate the aviation industry's demands. "As a first step we need to do all we possibly can to make the most of existing capacity. But on any view that is not enough. We have built the fourth largest economy in the world; air travel is crucial to our expanding economy."

Conservationists experienced a dreadful sense of deja vu. As far back as 1995, for instance, the Council for the Protection of Rural England (CPRE) said in evidence to the House of Commons Transport Committee: "Planning future capacity for air transport has, to date, been based on official forecasts of predicted growth in passenger numbers ... It is now recognised in a number of different sectors, such as energy and surface transport, that simply meeting predicted demand is neither achievable nor desirable. CPRE believes that future air transport policy should similarly aim to encourage the management of demand where environmental problems exist."

The CPRE complained that planning for air capacity "is conducted in a vacuum which does not consider the wider implications or alternatives in terms of other transport modes". For domestic and short-haul European flights, it was pointed out, high-speed rail links could provide a competitive alternative. Seven years later, the high-speed rail link from London to the Channel Tunnel remained unbuilt while the ricketyness of mainline rail journeys between London and Glasgow or Edinburgh forced serious business people onto air shuttles.

The environmental problems of cars, like danger, noise and pollution, are repeated in the skies. Noise indeed is even worse because aircraft are all-pervasive: in the crowded island of Britain there is hardly anywhere we can get away from them. From a roar on takeoff to a distant rumble high in the sky, they are always there.

Noisy planes are the modern equivalent of whip-cracking carters in Arthur Schopenhauer's day. The 19th century German philosopher hated noise and especially loathed whip-cracking: "The most inexcusable and disgraceful of all noises is the cracking of whips – a truly infernal thing when it is done in the narrow resounding streets of a town. I denounce it as making a peaceful life impossible."

He went on: "Hammering, the barking of dogs and the crying of children are horrible sounds; but your only genuine assassin of thought is the crack of a whip

... I really cannot see why a fellow who is taking away a waggon-load of gravel or dung should thereby obtain the right to kill in the bud the thoughts which may happen to be springing up in 10,000 heads – the number he will disturb one after the other in half an hour's drive through the town" (from his essay On Noise, in *Studies in Pessimism*). Mechanisation and motorisation have spread noise nuisance ever wider. A noisy or ill timed plane can annoy hundreds of thousands in the time it took Schopenhauer's carter to disturb 10,000.

Night flying from Heathrow Airport, London produced a distressingly high level of noise at Crystal Palace, 17 miles (27km) away, the Evening Standard found in an investigation. Against the standard threshold for noise annoyance of 57 decibels, at least five planes between 4.30am and 6.00am produced readings of more than 60 decibels. At the Oval, 14 miles (22km) from Heathrow, two aircraft hit 70 decibels before 5am. The newspaper commented that noise problems from Heathrow covered a much wider area than the government and the aircraft industry acknowledged.

Nor are the dead in a better position if they are interred in Brompton Cemetery, West London. It is under the Heathrow flight path.

The official British measure of aircraft noise, dBA (decibels) Leq, represents the equivalent continuous sound level. Aircraft noise over a 16-hour period (excluding night-time) at various monitoring points is averaged, and noise contour maps produced. These look rather like Ordnance Survey maps where contour lines represent the height of the ground. As a measure of community disturbance, 57 dBA Leq is seen as low, 63 Leq as medium and 69 Leq as high.

The index is a useful planning tool but it is not the total answer. Leq contours cannot be read as a reality in the way that hill contours can be. Hills do not move but planes change their direction of flight. Military jets and private planes criss-cross the sky far away from the contours surrounding commercial airports. The Leq level is an average, which is little help to individuals troubled by sudden bursts of sound. A single screeching hedge-hopping warplane can cause extreme anguish but will not alter the Leq level. In any case, reaction to aircraft noise is a personal thing: it varies from person to person and, with an individual, according to mood, state of health or even time of day.

Over the last four decades or so quieter aircraft have meant that the noise contours around some airports have actually shrunk. The Aviation Environment Federation and associated groups fear that the sheer increase in aircraft numbers will erode the benefits achieved so far. Nor would fewer, larger aircraft necessarily answer the problem because, under International Civil Aviation Organisation regulations, the heavier the plane the more noise it is allowed to make. The federation has complained about the practice of "hush-kitting" older planes to meet the current noise standard, known as Chapter 3. "This involves silencing the engine but the noise benefits are generally very marginal and their fitting frequently leads to an increase in emissions," the federation said.

An acceptable average noise level of 57 Leq and the "normal" urban background level of 40 Leq raise the question of how such a subjective experience as noise nuisance can be expressed meaningfully in measurable limits. The philosopher and the carter had very different ideas about acceptable noise!

Worse, a study in Austria suggested that typical urban noise levels affected children's health. They were found to have raised blood pressure, heart rates and levels of stress hormones. "Non-auditory effects of noise appear to occur at levels far below those required to damage hearing," said Peter Lercher of the University of Innsbruck. Presumably adults, too, may have difficulty in coping with our increasingly noisy society.

The extent of the noise issue is underlined by historian Jasper Ridley's observation that of 175 generations to have lived in Britain since civilisation was established, the most recent four are separated from the previous 171 by the loss of silence. The present period seems to have had the worst of it so far, with the country said to be three times noisier than it was 30 years ago. As prisoners we are embracing our chains, immersing ourselves in non-stop music or chatter and failing to notice external nuisances like overdriven cars and noisy planes.

As commercial aviation grows noise will increasingly be an issue across the country and not just for those beneath the flight path. Already, on the high and remote Pennines we can be alone with our thoughts, the wind and the birds – alone, that is, apart from the frequent drone of aircraft. This is the ultimate loss of silence.

A brave attempt to put quantitative flesh on the impressionistic bones of noise pollution was made by the Council for the Protection of Rural England and the Countryside Commission with their "tranquil areas" maps, published in 1995. These confirmed that huge swaths of the country were subjected to visual or noise intrusion as measured by a variety of "disturbing factors" (see below). The maps and accompanying analysis, presenting the situation in the early 1960s and the early 1990s, demonstrated how matters had worsened over the three decades.

Against a background of green representing tranquil areas free from urban intrusion, cities and towns are coloured grey and "semi-tranquil" areas are left white. The loss of green to white is particularly striking, so that the green areas of Sussex for example are being squeezed between London stretching south and the coastal developments stretching north. The maps underline the fact that the battle for the countryside is not only about stopping urban sprawl; it is also about curbing intrusive elements outside urban areas. A tranquil area, according to the compilers' criteria, lies

- *beyond military and civil airfield/airport noise lozenges as defined by published data where available (and also beyond very extensive opencast mining);*
- *4 km (2.5 miles) from the largest power stations;*
- *3 km (1.9 miles) from the busiest motorways, larger towns (Leicester and bigger) and major industrial areas;*
- *2 km (1.2 miles) from other motorways, major trunk roads and smaller towns;*
- *1 km (0.6 miles) from medium disturbance roads and some main railways.*

In the 1960s, 70 per cent (91,880 sq km, or 35,470 sq miles) of England was considered tranquil but by the 1990s this had shrunk to 56 per cent (73,012 sq km, or 28,180 sq miles). The loss was greatest in the South East, which suffered a 20 per cent drop leaving only 38 per cent of the region tranquil. More surprisingly, the next greatest loss of tranquillity (17 per cent) was found in the South West although two-thirds of the region (66 per cent) remained tranquil.

England's most peaceful county was Northumberland with 86 per cent tranquil areas in the 1990s, slipping from 91 per cent three decades earlier. The least peaceful were the West Midlands and Greater London conurbations, which nevertheless and surprisingly for big-city sprawls each managed one per cent tranquil areas.

The complete regional analysis, showing the proportion of tranquil areas in the early 1990s, is: North East 68 per cent; South West 66 per cent; East Anglia 64 per cent; Yorkshire and Humberside 60 per cent; East Midlands 56 per cent; West Midlands and North West both 55 per cent; South East 38 per cent.

The CPRE/Countryside Commission analysis also presented an England where tranquillity comes not in vast tracts but in pockets, and pockets of decreasing size. In the South East, with the smallest tranquil areas, the average size in the 1990s was 25 sq km (10 sq miles), down 77 per cent from 109 sq km (42 sq miles) three decades earlier. In the North East, with the largest tranquil areas, the comparable figures were 74 sq km (29 sq miles), down 42 per cent from 127 sq km (49 sq miles).

While the tranquil areas project was both innovatory and valuable, it nevertheless enshrines lowered expectations of noise and visual intrusion. We have lost the England where the absence of human sounds and the darkness of the night were the norms, presumably never to get it back. Air traffic and street lights colouring the sky for miles have seen to that.

Noise from planes using Gatwick Airport triggered a lawsuit decided by the House of Lords. In Farley v Skinner (October 2001) a house purchaser sued a surveying firm which allegedly failed to report that the property was affected by aircraft noise, although asked particularly to look into the matter. The claimant said he would not have bought the property if he had known how bad the noise was. The trial judge awarded him £10,000 damages. The verdict was reversed on appeal but restored in the House of Lords.

Typically, airport flight paths knock 15 per cent of the value of a home, the Daily Telegraph reported quoting a Hometrack survey. That puts aircraft noise up with "pungent takeaways" and late-night music venues as a nuisance. It is ahead of busy roads (12 per cent), electricity pylons (nine per cent), prisons (eight per cent) and railway lines (six per cent).

No-one knows more about noise and amenity issues surrounding airports than the Heathrow campaigning group HACAN Clear Skies. In October 2001 the group thought it had won a notable victory after a seven-year legal battle: the European Court of Human Rights ruled that people near the airport were entitled to sleep undisturbed between 11.30pm and 6.00am, which would mean a ban on the 16 or so flights that land at Heathrow during the night. The eight claimants, who were backed by several councils, were awarded £4,000 compensation each. One of the eight claimants – who moved to get away from the planes – later described the distress that he and his wife felt. John Cavalla said: "We used to lie in bed and be woken at 4.30am by the roar of the first flight. Then at 6am all hell would break loose and planes started landing every minute or so. It was an absolute nightmare and left us irritable for the rest of the day."

Philippa Edmunds, another of the eight, who has two young children, said: "Sleep deprivation is used as a form of torture. That is what happens when these jumbo jets start arriving at 4am and keep on coming. It is a human rights issue, the right to a decent night's sleep."

The European court ruled that night flights violated the residents' right to "respect for private and family life". It held that the British government had failed to strike a fair balance between business needs and the interests of local residents. A jubilant John Stewart, chairman of HACAN, said: "We are pretty confident that the government will respect this judgment and within 18 months we will see a ban on night flights." He was too optimistic. Soon afterwards the government appealed against the decision. The appeal was upheld, so for the long-suffering residents it was business as usual.

Apart from business lobbying, the government was no doubt aware of the prospect of having to pay up to £2 billion in compensation to residents affected by aircraft noise. According to HACAN, households in a band stretching from beyond Windsor in the west and across much of south London experience noise levels above the 57 decibels limit. This is an area that includes super-wealthy Richmond-upon-Thames and the Queen's weekend home, Windsor Castle, proving that aircraft noise is no respecter of money and rank.

While noisy aircraft are an aggravation 20 miles (32km) and more from the airport, residents of Ruislip enjoy untroubled skies barely seven miles (11km) away. The leafy suburb is north of Heathrow, whose runways are aligned east-west, so planes do not pass over Ruislip. Clearly the most tranquil spot is in the lee of a major airport.

Heathrow, always controversial, was back in the news in November 2001 when the government allowed a fifth terminal after an eight-year public inquiry. A cap on the number of aircraft movements which accompanied the decision did nothing to appease conservationists, who denounced Terminal Five as a "Trojan horse" for further airport expansion (which was duly proposed the following year). Under the cap annual movements were limited to 480,000, which were expected to mean 90 million passengers, compared with current levels of around 460,000 movements – a daily average of 1,260 – and 64 million passengers.

True to form at Heathrow, the latest cap was soon under challenge. The Department for Transport's strategic framework, *The Future of Air Transport*, published in December 2003, raised the prospect of ending runway alternation at peak hours. This is a system that reduces noise disturbance for people living under the flight paths in West London. Ending it, according to HACAN, would take annual flight movements over the 480,000 limit.

Heathrow has a habit of making nonsense of projections as the appetite for air travel continues unabated. In 1979 the public inquiry into a fourth terminal set a limit of 260,000 movements a year.

In 1992 even the airport's owner, BAA, could not get it right. At that time the airport was dealing with 410,000 movements and 50 million passengers a year. BAA, which was expecting larger aircraft that did not materialise, wanted a cap of 453,000 movements, which figure it expected to be reached in 2016. Instead, the figure was reached in less than half the time. From 1992, when Terminal Five was first proposed, passengers increased by 28 per cent and aircraft movements by 13 per cent in less than a decade, with every sign that growth will continue.

The noise problem is greatly increased by military flying. Military exercises need space, leading to the sad irony that many of the least populated and most tranquil parts of the country are the worst affected by obtrusive planes. North Wales, East Anglia, the Borders and Scotland's Western Isles are all affected.

The RAF has around 400 aircraft (December 2002) excluding helicopters, trainers and smaller transport planes, based at 13 stations around the United Kingdom. They include 156 combat-version Tornados, 56 Harriers and 46 Jaguars plus 50 of the giant Hercules transport planes. There are 98 helicopters, excluding the Merlin HC3 in course of delivery.

America has scaled down its military presence in Britain since the end of the cold war, but as well as various intelligence-gathering sites it has the US Air Force 48th Fighter Wing at Lakenheath, Suffolk. This base contains almost 5,000 military personnel and an unspecified number of F15E Strike Eagle planes and the older F15C Eagle. Lakenheath is the USAF's only F15 fighter wing in Europe.

Jonny Beardsall of the Daily Telegraph wrote about a flight with Wing Commander Andy Sudlow of the RAF's 16 Squadron, based at Lossiemouth. The wingco explained that low-level flying, vital in wartime if planes are to avoid enemy radar, missiles and guns, was a "perishable skill" that each Jaguar pilot had to practise for 250 hours a year. An aircraft could normally fly no closer than 250ft (76m) to the ground, but in designated training areas this could drop to 100ft (30m) provided the noise on the ground did not exceed 125 decibels. *(This is more than double the official threshold level for annoyance from noise.)*

Most low-flying took place over thinly populated areas. "You take tremendous trouble to avoid villages, but it's impossible to miss every house." Among places never to be overflown were a riding centre for the disabled, hospitals with psychiatric patients and those performing microsurgery, and nuclear power stations. Some areas were avoided on a seasonal basis, from a nest of ospreys to the Cairngorms ski slopes in winter.

"There isn't an RAF pilot that I know who would break the rules of our own accord," said Wing Cdr Sudlow. "We are all conscious of bad publicity and of the difficulty of getting people to accept what we do."

Despite their respect for the RAF, Darby and Catherine Dennis were unable to accept what the RAF does above their mansion near Stamford. Over many years their lives were made "unbearable" by Harrier jets on training flights. The value of the house reportedly more than halved because of the noise. In April 2003, the couple were awarded £950,000 in damages from the Ministry of Defence. The court, however, made no order for the flights to stop. Mr Dennis said the effect of noise was "aggravated by its persistence and, to an extent, its unpredictability". The magazine Aircraft Illustrated talked to an unnamed Strike Eagle pilot from Lakenheath. The US pilot said Britain "has the best low altitude and mountainous training airspace in most of the world". In an apparent reference to public feelings about low flying, he commented: "I truly feel that the efforts of the United Kingdom governments [sic] will continue to aid in the preparation of its military aviators. I appreciate the sacrifices the people of the UK make so that its defenders of freedom can be their very best."

Military pilots occasionally kill themselves but rarely others in the air unless they mean to. The safety of civilian aircraft is increasingly an issue, however. In July 2002, a midair collision over Germany between a Russian airliner and a cargo plane, which killed 71 including 45 children, focused attention on civilian safety in Britain's crowded skies. Public concern was heightened by long-running system and financing problems at National Air Traffic Services, which controls airspace over the UK and the eastern North Atlantic. NATS handles two million flights a year – a daily average of almost 5,500 flights. Despite the German tragedy, the British air traffic control insisted that "safety levels have never been higher" and said near-misses, known as "risk-bearing aircraft proximity events (Airprox)", attributable to NATS were at an all-time low of 0.3 per 100,000 movements (.0003 per cent). It gave these figures: 1995, 12; 1996, 16; 1997, 11; 1998, six; 1999, five; 2000, six.

Despite NATS' ritual declaration that safety will never be compromised, that is the only construction that can be put on a decision by the pan-European air traffic control agency, buffeted by the public's unceasing demands to fit in ever-more flights. Common sense says that halving the vertical separation between planes increases the risk of an Airprox, or even a collision, but that is what Eurocontrol has allowed: above 29,000ft (8,840m) – the level at which typical cruising heights start – planes need only stay 1,000ft (305m) apart instead of 2,000ft (610m) as before.

The predict and provide approach gives the rulers of Europe's skies an impossible task. Amid existing worries about overcrowded skies, the government has countenanced a huge rise in passengers using British airports. Air traffic controllers are left trying to square the circle of safety and demand. The DfT's consultation document said "the difficulties are not insuperable" in meeting increased demand safely. This less than ringing expression of confidence was based on a number of "capacity-enhancing tools" being in place by 2010. They include more precise tracking and separation of aircraft on departure routes, and multiple closely spaced departure and en-route procedures. At this point anyone who has been at an airport when the package holidays change over will say, "Oh yes!" The danger is clear: that we shall be committed to more flights without the certainty that they can be safely handled.

The CPRE, in a 2001 submission to the government on the future of aviation, explained Britain's crowded skies as a legacy of empire, by which the country "accommodates a disproportionate amount of the world's international travel and as such carries a disproportionate environmental burden". The "historically unrestrained growth of the aviation industry" should be replaced, the conservation body argued, with sustainable growth based on demand management, environmental constraints, and integrated transport and land use policies. It was made clear that the aviation industry simply isn't paying its environmental way: it has a special exemption from fuel duty and is also exempted, like other public transport, from value-added tax on travel tickets.

The CPRE posed the question If aviation covers its environmental costs, should capacity then be provided to meet demand? and answered, somewhat equivocally, "Since by their very nature environmental costs can never be fully recovered, the government and the industry must seek to mitigate and reduce the [environmental] costs of air travel".

If this document was speaking softly to policymakers in their own circuitous language, the Aviation Environment Federation's booklet *Flying Into Trouble*, whose backers included the CPRE, Transport 2000 and Friends of the Earth, put the environmental case more plainly. "Meeting predicted demand will require the equivalent of a new airport the current size of Stansted every year for the next 30 years. This scale of growth is simply unsustainable; to promote it is hugely irresponsible," the booklet declared.

It claimed that Britain has potential extra airport capacity for which planning permission has been given of between 62 and 80 million passengers a year. *Flying Into Trouble* argued that if air travel grew until 2030 at the same rate as road traffic "the UK's 'capacity problem' immediately disappears; existing planning approvals could cater for all that demand". The comparison with road traffic was surely the green equivalent of the medical principle that a big pain drives out a smaller pain!

Flying Into Trouble complained that the government's approach, "however dressed up", remained that of predict and provide. It argued that demand could be managed by a combination of:

— *eliminating the aviation industry's hidden and distorting subsidies;*
— *charging realistic market price for landing slots at airports (elsewhere, greens argue for capacity auctions);*

> — *ensuring that aviation fully meets its environ-*
> *mental and social costs;*
> — *encouraging passengers to transfer from air to*
> *rail for some domestic and Continental jour-*
> *neys;*
> — *not permitting capacity increases where these*
> *breach environmental limits, and where provid-*
> *ing them would result in unacceptable environ-*
> *mental and social impacts.*

The environmental campaign group Transport 2000, in a policy statement, called for aviation to be subject to the same sustainability constraints as road travel. It wanted clear strategies "for reducing the rate of growth, and ultimately the level, of air travel". To manage demand, T2000 urged the promotion of rail as a substitute for shorter distance flights, the taxation of aviation fuel, the phasing out of duty free concessions and limits on growth in airport capacity. It also sought tougher overall limits on airport noise and pollution emissions.

The consultation document implied, and the white paper a year later confirmed, that aviation growth will continue the let-it-rip approach of roads and housing – the origin of the endless ribbon development along the South Coast and the grim conurbations of Lancashire and Yorkshire. After a period in official disfavour – with housing dating back at least to the seminal Town and Country Planning Act – the approach is all too alive again with a spate of new motorway building and green belts under severe building pressures.

The M25 London orbital motorway was originally built to relieve congestion in central London, but the road rapidly became congested itself while leaving congestion in the centre untouched. It became clear that the M25 was attracting a lot of new traffic on journeys that would otherwise not have been made.

For years the M25 was seen as the ultimate demonstration that we cannot build our way out of congestion. It still is, although the lesson has been studiously unlearned by current decision-makers. The more-the-merrier approach to roads was pounded back to life with the July 2003 plan to turn the M25 into an eight-lane so-called superhighway, with 12 lanes in the Heathrow area.

The M6 toll motorway, which opened in December 2003, is a 27-mile (44km) route in the Birmingham area intended to relieve congestion on the original M6. The launch price for cars using the privately owned motorway was £2. Any relief is likely to be short-lived except to the extent that tolls are progressively raised to create a "road for the rich". Transport 2000 called it a "white elephant", with respite from traffic jams set to be quickly cancelled out by rising traffic levels due to the release of suppressed demand.

Spokesman Steve Hounsham said: "Birmingham's green belt has been sacrificed in vain because in five years' time congestion will be back to normal. The only difference will be there will be two roads full of traffic moving through the area in the place of one."

Even more than the motorways, airport expansion brings problems of "land take". As well as by the airport itself, land is consumed by the supporting infrastructure of access roads and railways, warehouses and offices, and housing. In England's green and pleasant land there is scarcely anywhere ugly enough that a major airport could be sited there without drawing protests about the destruction of landscape and rural life. The cultural threat of an airport understandably causes as much anguish as more health-threatening but less visible issues.

Behind the growth of air travel is the great British package holiday, and more recently the continental mini-break. Scarred by the great fuel and fox-hunting protests, ministers know that on certain issues they mess with the public at their peril. We cannot have holidays in Spain, Cyprus and Florida, not to mention Australia, Thailand and the Caribbean, without airports and planes. On this issue no-one is simon-pure: we are all polluters now. This business represents money out of the country: Benidorm's gain is Blackpool's loss. Much of the holiday spend ends up in the pockets of foreign hoteliers, bar owners and tour operators.

Although offset by foreign visitors to Britain, Grayling and Bishop's *Sustainable Aviation 2030* (described earlier in the chapter) put the deficit in tourism expenditure in 1999 at £7bn and rising. (By 2002, the annual deficit had risen to more than double that figure.)

The authors said the link between air transport and productivity growth was more readily assumed than proved, and therefore there was "serious concern" about predictions of future economic losses due to capacity constraint. They called for the "prudent" expansion of air transport, which was neither the unconstrained growth sought by much of the aviation industry nor the zero growth wanted by some green groups.

Airlines are able to draw in passengers with cheap fares partly because they do not pay tax on fuel – even though aircraft are big producers of the main greenhouse gas, carbon dioxide. A passenger flying from London to Florida generates as much CO_2 as a typical motorist in a year. The average output of CO_2 from a passenger aircraft is 170g per passenger per kilometre (pkm) compared with 60g/pkm for a diesel express train and 20g/pkm for a long-distance coach. Some car models produce even more CO_2 per kilometre. The Ferrari 456GTA, according to Britain's Vehicle Certification Agency, records 570g per km. This, though, is per car not per passenger. And even Ferraris do not usually travel hundreds or thousands of miles in a trip. Which leaves airliners in a class of their own as polluters.

Military flying has disproportionate environmental effects. In separate studies quoted by the Royal Commission on Environmental Pollution, 18 per cent of the world's military/commercial aircraft fleet were military in 1992, but at around that time military aircraft used about one-third of the fuel of the commercial fleet. The number of military planes was predicted to fall to seven per cent of the total by 2015, although this estimate was made before the West's heightened terror awareness from September 2001 onwards. The commission pointed out that military planes produce proportionately more pollutants than civil aircraft, particularly oxides of nitrate. This chemical released into the stratosphere reduces ozone, and thus affects climate.

Aircraft were responsible for 3.5 per cent of man-made outputs affecting climate in 1992, the United Nations' Intergovernmental Panel on Climate Change (IPCC) estimated in *Aviation and the Global Atmosphere* (1999). This "radiative forcing", when introduced activities affect the natural balance between radiation from the sun and thermal radiation from the earth, was predicted to increase to five per cent by 2050. Supersonic aircraft are particularly heavy polluters: the report pointed out that supersonic aircraft have a radiative forcing effect five times greater than their subsonic equivalents.

Among the difficulties of predicting environmental pollution in the future, two certainties may be stated. While most of the world is committed to reducing carbon dioxide emissions overall, aviation – an important source of those emissions – is heading in the opposite direction: it is set to keep on growing. Secondly, aircraft are disproportionately heavy polluters compared with other human activities. *Aviation and the Global Atmosphere* found that subsonic aircraft produced overall radiative forcing two to four times greater than the forcing effect from CO_2 alone. This compares with the total radiative forcing from all human activities, which is only half as much again as that due to CO_2.

The respected Royal Commission on Environmental Pollution, in its report *The Environmental Effects of Civil Aircraft in Flight* (November 2002), showed that the impact of aircraft on climate change is even greater than widely supposed since the IPCC put the issue into the public realm in 1992. Between 1992 and 2000, the royal commission said, aviation distances travelled increased by 43 per cent and fuel used by 33 per cent – respectively, about five per cent and four per cent annually. These were at the high end of the IPCC's expectations.

The commission did not believe that changes in engine design and other technical improvements would by themselves provide a solution to environmental problems because their effect was likely to be outstripped by the rise in air traffic. In any case, it commented strikingly, "two thirds of all the aircraft that will be flying in 2030 are already in use". ·

Aircraft emissions described in *The Environmental Effects of Civil Aircraft in Flight* included carbon dioxide, oxides of nitrogen, water vapour and particles (mainly from sulphur oxides). These all affect the climate. CO_2 contributes directly to global warming while aircraft condensation trails (contrails) composed of water vapour and particles are increasingly thought to influence temperature change indirectly through the formation of cirrus clouds. These clouds reflect solar radiation back towards space – and have a cooling effect on the ground – but also absorb thermal radiation from the surface and re-emit it downwards. The warming effect on the ground is believed to dominate*.

A dramatic illustration of the possible effect of contrails was provided after the September 11, 2001 terror attacks in the United States, when commercial aircraft were grounded for three days. Contributors to the science journal Nature (quoted by the commission) reported that in the absence of contrails there was a one-two deg C increase in the day-night temperature difference across the country.

Oxides of nitrogen from aircraft flying at typical subsonic heights increase the amount of ozone, which shields the earth from excessive solar radiation, but at supersonic heights the effect is reversed so that emissions reduce ozone. The commission reiterated the IPCC's warning that supersonic flights have particularly damaging climatic effects.

The commission said it was "deeply concerned at the prospect of continuing rapid increases in air transport" and consequences for greenhouse gas emissions. Since aviation fuel is tax-exempt airlines are receiving "in effect as large subsidy at the expense of other modes of transport or sectors and the environment". This also made it harder for the United Kingdom, as a signatory to the 1997 Kyoto Protocol, to meet its commitment to reducing greenhouse gas emissions by 2012.

The commission recognised that unpicking the web of bilateral agreements over tax-free fuel was not prac-

---

* The effect is complex, however. The eminent climatologist Sir John Houghton says that in general for high clouds the warming effect dominates while for low clouds it is the cooling effect. Other factors are the nature and size of the cloud particles and the thickness of the cloud. (*Global Warming: the Complete Briefing*, Cambridge, 2nd ed 1997)

ticable, but urged a Europe-wide emissions charge on aircraft as a way of restraining the growth of passenger and freight flights. It declared: "The availability of cheap air transport currently enjoyed by the public is a very recent phenomenon. It is not a traditional 'right' in any sense." Those attached to their cheapie holidays, even if at the expense of the environment, could take heart from the fact that British governments have a long history of ignoring the reports of royal commissions.

Among possible demand management measures, the commission described how restricting slots at airports would encourage airlines to concentrate on the more profitable and relatively less polluting longer distances. Aviation should be included in the Kyoto carbon trading system – the permits to pollute. However, because radiative forcing represents about three times the level of CO_2 produced "the aviation industry should acquire three carbon emission permits for each unit of carbon that it actually emits".

When the Department for Transport published its ideas about airport expansion, residents in the affected areas were quick to react. Outside the British Airways headquarters at Heathrow an un-British scuffle broke out between protesters and security staff. The protesters were angry that a formal consultation exercise was being run on an invitation-only basis. Pushing and shoving lasted for 10 minutes until the police arrived.

In Harmondsworth, next to Heathrow, protesters pressed into use signs on poles left over from the previous year's general election. The signs were re-erected with No Third Runway posters pasted over the Vote Labour message – a nicely ironic although apparently unintended way of letting the world know what the protesters thought about the government of the day.

British Airways, privately owned but the nation's flag carrier, pressed hard to expand Heathrow, with the airline "not interested in anywhere else" in Britain, according to John Stewart, chair of the campaigning group HACAN Clear Skies. BA, he believed, saw the third Heathrow runway as "the only realistic option for maintaining an internationally competitive aviation hub in Britain". It was a sentiment that spoke to a government concerned about airport competition from Paris, Amsterdam and Frankfurt.

John Stewart is strongly opposed to a third runway at Heathrow and is no nimby either: he does not want new runways anywhere. He says demand management and not unbridled capacity is the way to go. He challenges the idea that airport expansion is about meeting business needs or about liberating poorer people to fly.

Stewart's group, HACAN Clear Skies, says business trips make up only 24 per cent of journeys by plane but even if this rose to 30 per cent as predicted by the British government the increased number of trips "could be easily accommodated by existing airport capacity" (*It's The Economy, Stupid,* February 2003).

"Short-term leisure travel is where the expansion will come," Stewart says. "The government seems to accept that it's not its business to stop people flying, but this will benefit mainly the well-to-do. The country's top 10 per cent of earners will be taking six or seven weekend breaks a year [if demand is not regulated]."

In 2002 (the latest available year), UK residents made 59.4 million visits abroad, with holidays overwhelmingly (two-thirds) the main reason. Visits to friends and relatives accounted for another 13 per cent. Business trips were a meagre 14 per cent. The growth of holiday travel averaged more than five per cent annually for the five years 1998-2002.

The figures, from the International Passenger Survey published by the British government's Office of National Statistics (ONS), are for all modes of travel, but air was by far the main mode.

Overseas visitors to the UK in 2002 made far fewer trips – 24.2 million – but with a much more even spread in the main reasons for travel: holiday 32 per cent, business 30 per cent, visits to friends and relatives 26 per cent.

The extent to which spending is being exported – and hence jobs lost in Britain – is underlined by a remorseless trend in the travel statistics. The balance of payments travel account has been in deficit (ie, UK residents spent more abroad than overseas visitors spent in Britain) since 1996. It has risen each year from that time to its current, record annual level of £15.2 billion.

Short-term leisure travel doesn't come shorter or more leisurely than groups from Britain who descend on Prague for stag weekends aided by budget flights reportedly costing as little as £18. Many men are already drunk when they arrive in the beautiful Baroque city for "cheap sex and cheap beer" visits. One bar manager complained that the stag groups "dribble into their beers and generally lower our standards". At least the Britons have shaken off the football hooligan reputation. A police inspector said: "They are more pleasant drunk than the German are when they're sober." Just typical beneficiaries of cheap flights? Freedom-to-fly campaigners would find it tough to argue that the human rights of such groups would be infringed if flights became more expensive and they had to descend instead on British coastal resorts.

Nor for more sophisticated UK travellers would life be unsupportable without a weekend trip to the Masai Mara, Kenya, or a day trip to a Norwegian fjord to see whales – yet in 2003-04 both were on offer.

The way that available flights create demand is well illustrated by the case of Matt Lewis and Nicky Bates, a young couple living near Stansted Airport. They told the Channel 4 TV programme A Place In The Sun that they were spending £70,000 on a holiday home in Costa del Azabar, Spain, which they could reach for weekend breaks. Nicky explained that, beyond going to restaurants and pubs, they were "not making much use of our disposable income".

When the DfT published its consultation document suggesting a possible third runway at Heathrow, Father Phil Hughes, the priest in charge at the affected villages of Harmondsworth, Sipson and Longford, stood by his parishioners in the seemingly David-and-Goliath fight.

"I love aviation, but the community is distraught by the runway proposal," said the Anglican clergyman. "It affects homes, schools, spiritual life. It is wiping history off the map."

Father Phil, also a chaplain at Heathrow Airport, hoped that the seemingly opposite demands of industry and community could be reconciled. "We have to increase capacity and remain competitive," he said. "But planes are getting bigger as well as quieter. With up to 800 in a plane we may not need new runways at all."

This idea has looked like more than a pious hope since the announcement of the Airbus A380. This double-decker super-jumbo, due in service in 2006, has a capacity for 800 passengers (although immediately a seating configuration of 550 is expected.)

Heathrow is the world's busiest airport for international flights and its second busiest cargo port. The off-balance sheet price of the third runway puts at risk the picturesque village of Harmondsworth with its 11th century church, medieval great barn and 16th century pub, the Five Bells.

For Stansted, buried in beautiful Essex countryside, the impact of a new runway would be no less dramatic. The airport came into operation after years of bitter argument, and in 1991 was handling just 1.5 million passengers. By 2002 this was 14 million. The consultation document floated the idea of three new runways allowing the airport to handle 80 million passengers annually. Its 756,000 aircraft movements would exceed Heathrow's.

Norman Mead, a veteran campaigner and chairman of Stop Stansted Expansion campaign, said: "Three runways – it is the work of madmen. We are facing the loss of the heritage of this part of the country. We are facing everything. More noise. More pollution. Increased risk of accidents. People will fight tooth and nail against it. Lying down in front of bulldozers and that sort of thing is foreign to us, but we shall see."

Peter Carter-Ruck, a resident near Stansted, argued in the Daily Telegraph that local people must be spared from yet more noise intrusion, and the answer was to locate a new airport offshore. He was answered three days later by Conservative politician Mark Reckless, who spoke up for Cliffe, in the Kent marshes, who evidently thought the idea was aimed at him. Mr Reckless suggested in effect that people near Stansted and Heathrow should just get on with it: an airport at Cliffe, where none presently existed, would be "qualitatively worse than what he [Mr Carter-Ruck] describes, since its impact on those living nearby would be revolutionary rather than evolutionary".

The Cliffe proposal would also badly affect an important wildlife site. Other people wanted to send the airport over the cliff and site it not close to the Thames Estuary but in it (also opposed by bird lovers). Area residents have been there before with a rejected plan to build an airport on Maplin Sands.

For the villagers of Church Lawford near Rugby, the prospect of a giant airport – bigger than the present capacity of Heathrow – in this arcadia so handy for the towns of the West Midlands conurbation cast an immediate pall on property prices. Soon after the airport plan emerged out of a clear blue sky, a local estate agent said of house sales in the villages affected: "There is no market."

Manchester was earmarked for possible major expansion. It already has the appetite for growth. Although Manchester is often seen simply as one of Britain's regional airports, the magazine Aircraft Illustrated found (March 2000) that it was among the world's 20 busiest airports, with 17 million passengers a year plus cargo flights. More than 90 airlines served around 175 destinations, producing more than 600 aircraft movements a day. Even before the government consultation document, the airport was forecast to see 30 million passengers a year by 2007 and 40 million by 2015. Manchester's rate of growth has "alarmed both environmentalists and local community groups", the magazine said.

Days before the planned end of the consultation period on November 30, 2002, the government was hit by two bombshells. With just one day to go, and with an embargo on information being released in advance, the Royal Commission on Environmental Pollution produced its report *The Environmental Effects of Civil Aircraft in Flight*. This heavily stressed the climatic risks of aviation growth. The effect was to make the government look heedless in the face of the commission's detailed argumentation that aircraft activity has an even greater impact than supposed. And three days before that, a high court judge overturned the government's decision to leave Gatwick out of the consultation. This meant an extension of the consultation period and of the uncertainties over where airport expansion would take place.

Residents around Gatwick, the second biggest London airport, thought they had reason to be grateful for a 1979 legal agreement between the county council and the airport operator, barring a second runway there until 2019. On the basis of that the Department for Transport, to its credit, did not include Gatwick in the consultation document. However, objectors sought to dilute the chances of their areas being chosen by exporting their misfortunes.

This display of nimbyism involved Kent and Medway councils, whose jurisdictions include Cliffe; Essex County Council, whose area includes Stansted; and Norman Mead (the airport campaigner) and David Fossett, both residents of the Stansted area. The objectors did not include the airport operator, BAA, or any airline.

The objectors' victory at the judicial review meant that Gatwick was now to be included in the consultation process, which in turn delayed the white paper to the end of 2003.

Mr Justice Kay's ruling did not affect the final decision about which airports would be expanded. Nor did it overturn the 1979 agreement, although he made clear that there were legal ways of doing this without the agreement of the contracting parties. He ruled that Gatwick should be included in the consultation as a matter of "rationality" and "fairness". It was not rational to exclude Gatwick because, among other reasons, even if the 1979 agreement was to run its course about a third of the 30-year period would remain and, in any event, the consultation document was open to the possibility of an increase in runway capacity at one or more of the other locations during that third decade. It was "procedurally unfair" because the claimants would probably and legitimately wish to advocate Gatwick as an alternative solution at a later stage in the decision-making process, yet the consultation was "their only real opportunity to present their case on Gatwick without there being in place a government policy which, realistically, will present them with an insurmountable hurdle".

Gatwick area residents heard the ruling with astonishment and fury. But in law matters are seldom as clearcut as they seem to the lay person. It was a hard lesson that most things can be undone or got round. It sent a signal to protesters everywhere that they are better off fighting to the finish because deals can be unpicked later. For older campaigners the Gatwick decision was an example of the creeping expansionism that has afflicted Stansted and London City airport. Be careful what you agree to because it won't end there!

For the Essex objectors it turned out to be an empty victory. Gatwick was included in the Department for Transport's final plans as a possible runway location from 2019 – but Stansted was the DfT's choice for the first new runway. (The Cliffe option was dropped.)

Messrs Mead and Fossett also made claims under two parts of the Human Rights Act, 1998: Article 8 (1) (respect for private life, home and correspondence), and Article 1 of the First Protocol (peaceful enjoyment of possessions). Although both submissions failed, the case is interesting as a marker for complaints about aircraft intrusion. Many more such cases can be expected.

The DfT suffered another setback early in the new year of 2003 when the Observer leaked a forthcoming report from the Institute for Public Policy Research, which it described as "New Labour's favourite think tank". It said the report, by Simon Bishop, called for plans for new runways to be abandoned while existing capacity was able to be used more efficiently. Measures would include auctioning landing slots and increased landing charges. The report said: "The key point is the Government must understand the climate change impact of future aviation growth ... Other industries are already footing the bill. The aviation industry is outside that. [There is no tax on aviation fuel or value added tax on airline transactions.] Other industries are effectively subsidising aviation."

The report slammed the government for being "in hock" to the aviation industry, according to the Observer.

While, all over the country, everybody found reasons for new runways and new airports to be somewhere else (when they weren't arguing for no more runways at all), mother-of-three Kerry Rawlings, in a letter front-paged by the Uxbridge Gazette, said the Heathrow plans had left her "heartbroken and horri-fied". She voiced her anguish at how noise and pollu-tion would affect her seven-year-old son, with a history of ill health, how she feared her home was just beyond the limit for compulsory compensation and how nobody would want to buy it because the area would become "ghost towns and villages".

"How do I explain to my children that it does not matter how hard you work, the government has the power to take your home, livelihood, and indeed health away from you?" she wrote.

Mrs Rawlings ended with an insight that has escaped the nation's six-figure policymakers: "If there is no alternative that is agreeable to the people in the whole of the country then we should manage with what we have got!"

FOUR
RUNWAYS AND THE
BLIGHTING OF BRITAIN

THE Department for Transport published its white paper, *The Future of Air Transport*, on December 16, 2003 – one day before the centenary of the Wright Brothers taking to the air for mankind's first powered, controlled flight. It approved new runways at Stansted, Heathrow, Birmingham and Edinburgh with two more possible runways, and new terminals and other expansion at airports around the country.

For greens, the plans were about as bad as they could be, particularly the absence of any attempt to limit growing travel demand. Or indeed a recognition of the need to do so. Instead, the government was determined that "over time" (a weasel phrase) the price of air travel "reflects its environmental and social impacts"*, which is not at all the same thing.

The DfT had simply taken the high growth scenario from its earlier consultation document and sought ways to meet it, to the tune of 470 million passengers per annum (mppa) by 2030. Of two immediately avail-

---

* What price do you put on polluted air or aircraft noise or land concreted over for airport development? Making the aviation industry pay for its so-called external costs only has value if the environmental and social impacts are lessened or removed. Yet the white paper makes clear that the industry has great capacity for absorbing costs without affecting growth. If the environmental and social impacts are not lessened or removed, charging is simply a revenue-raising device or a way for the government to go through the motions of taking action

able measures to dampen demand, an increase in air passenger duty was ruled out and the introduction of value added tax on tickets and other airline transactions was not mentioned.

Here then was predict and provide which even the DfT's own consultation document of 2002 had seemed to warn against!

The white paper stressed the need to balance the economic growth produced by aviation with environmental and social factors, particularly noise. It acknowledged that noise at night "is widely regarded as the least acceptable aspect of aircraft operations". The consultation launched in 2002 had "underlined the significance of aircraft noise as a key environmental impact in the public mind".

Economic considerations were never far away, however. "We will bear down on night noise accordingly, but we must strike a fair balance between local disturbance, the limits of social acceptability and the economic benefits of night flights."

The white paper was long on environmental rhetoric, but short on specifics. It stressed that local initiatives, industry support and technology changes were needed to address the problems. Emissions trading was the one substantial way in which the government sought to show it would deliver on its green pledges.

Emissions trading allocates to various industries a permitted quantity of carbon dioxide (or CO_2 equivalents) emissions. Within this amount, cleaner airlines would be able to sell spare quota to airlines that would otherwise exceed their quota. This is considered an incentive to airlines to clean up their act. But it also leaves richer airlines able to buy their way out of difficulty.

(The morality of such schemes is even more difficult when applied to countries. A rich country, say the

United States, can buy "permits to pollute" from poor countries, whose capacity for industrial development is then restricted because of lower emissions capacity.)

Whatever the morality, emissions trading is attractive as a policy instrument because, in the white paper's words, "it guarantees the desired environmental outcome in a way that other instruments, such as charges, do not".

The EU scheme is to start in 2005, running alongside similar schemes under the Kyoto accord. Aviation is not included in this first phase – given its propensity to pollute, we can ask why – but might be included in the second phase, from 2008. This is not guaranteed, however.

Press reports personalised the runway proposals as transport secretary Alistair Darling's decisions. They are better seen as the Department for Transport up to its old tricks of wanting to build things, although Darling was no doubt happy to avoid the political burden of saying no to limitless flights.

The minister said it is not his business to stop people flying, but the left-wing Daily Mirror – read by less well-to-do people who would be most affected by price rises to limit demand – pointed out that cheap flights come at a price.

The newspaper said: "The price of today's cheap flights will be paid by tomorrow's generations [in environmental pollution].

"It would be a bold government which put green considerations before the demands of travellers and the air industry. But we are entitled to expect better than another capitulation to the easiest solution." (The Mirror was perhaps referring to the widening of the M25 and other motorway works announced earlier in the year.)

Meanwhile, transport commentator Toby Moore, writing in the Times, wondered who these poor people are that the transport secretary does not want to price out of the air: three-quarters of the passengers for low-cost airlines are ABC1s (professionals and managers).

Moore wrote: "It might be churlish to wonder why the same regard is not given to the forms of travel that the poor actually do use. Bus and rail fares have risen by 42 per cent and 35 per cent respectively in real terms since 1984.

"The opportunity to fly cheaply is only one source of pleasure in life. There is also the right to sleep peacefully, to breathe clean air and travel easily across your own country rather than to another."

The Future of Air Transport rejected all suggested new airports, including those at Rugby (Church Lawford) and Cliffe. This at least was a benefit. The DfT preferred to develop many of the existing airports in all parts of the United Kingdom. A programme of terminal expansion and runway extensions underlay the headline-grabbing plan for between four and six new runways.

The first of the new runways, expected by 2011 or 2012, was at Stansted. This would increase the airport's capacity from an estimated 19mppa in 2003 to around 80mppa. A key advantage as seen by the white paper was that noise impact (since the airport is in a rural area) would be less than for the alternatives.

The government would not promote or pay for the £4 billion Stansted runway – raising the issue of who will. Heathrow-based airlines would resent paying for a runway they have little or no use for. Meanwhile, possible private investors might wonder about the business prospects of London's number three airport, miles farther away from the capital than Heathrow.

A third runway at Heathrow (shorter than the other two) was considered to generate the greatest economic benefits of any runway option, but was put back to

2015-2020 because of air pollution around the airport, especially nitrogen dioxide (NO_2) and particulates. The date was not set solely out of concern for residents' health but by the knowledge that an expanded Heathrow was unlikely to meet the EU's mandatory NO_2 limits due in 2010.

From 2015 "there would be a substantially better prospect of avoiding exceedences [sic]". The DfT, in other words, was gambling on future technology, leaving local residents in limbo as to whether the runway will be built.

The air pollution at Heathrow is made worse by the M25 and M4 motorways nearby. The M25 is the road that this same DfT is planning to expand to 12 lanes in the airport area.

Noise restrictions, said the white paper, should be applied so that the 57 dBA noise contour would be no larger than in summer 2002, when it was 127 sq km (49 square miles).

Extra capacity to be achieved by the third runway was not stated.

Expansion at Gatwick was influenced by an agreement between BAA, the airport operator, and West Sussex County Council, ruling out a second runway until 2019. A new runway to be built after that date would be considered if the Heathrow pollution problems were not overcome, said the white paper. While understandable as a fallback position, the effect is to blight properties for years to come. The same applies to the possible runway at Glasgow (see below).

This "generalised blight" occurs long before statutory remedies come into effect. According to the white paper, airport operators will be offering non-statutory schemes to address the problem.

The runway option preferred for Gatwick would increase annual passenger capacity to 83 million, up 40 million from the present level.

The Future of Air Transport did nothing to redress the concentration of airport capacity in the South East, which has such serious consequences for quality of life in that region. It also means that passengers from elsewhere in the country spend unnecessary hours going to and from the London airports.

One of the stated reasons for rejecting a new airport between Coventry and Rugby (Church Lawford) was that "significant constraints [would be] imposed on airport capacity in the South East", as if that would be a bad thing. Instead, a shortened runway for Birmingham International was chosen with the condition that it should not be used at night – a proviso that looks born to die.

Manchester, with two existing runways, is the only credible contender for a second UK hub airport, after Heathrow. The white paper noted the possibility, but proposed no steps to bring this about. It said Manchester, where another terminal was proposed, was using easily less than half its capacity – 19 million passengers a year against at least 50mppa.

The proposed runway at Birmingham, midway between Manchester and London, will make the emergence of Manchester as a hub less likely.

The government acknowledged noise concerns at Manchester, where 70,000 people might find themselves within the 57 dBA noise contour by 2030*. However, this is less than the number accepted for Birmingham, where 81,000 are expected to be within that contour in 2020.

A former submariner, Bryan Smalley, in a letter to the Daily Telegraph, well expressed the case for a Northern hub airport. In the 1960s he was told to take his boat on a courtesy visit to Manchester (surely one of the world's unlikeliest locations for a submarine). When he asked why, he was told that half the popula-

---

* The dBA (decibels) measure greatly understates the number of people troubled by aircraft noise. See discussion in previous chapter

THE FUTURE OF AIR TRANSPORT
MAIN PROPOSALS

New runways

Stansted	**2012**
Birmingham	**2016**
Heathrow (subject to pollution limits)	**2015-20**
Gatwick – poss (alternative to Heathrow third runway)	**after 2019**
Edinburgh	**2020**
Glasgow – poss	**by 2030**

Runway extensions

Bristol, Leeds/Bradford, Newcastle, Teesside, Liverpool John Lennon (poss)

Terminals

6th Heathrow terminal

Terminal development at Manchester and many other airports

New airports rejected

No new airports at Cliffe, Rugby, Alconbury, Central Scotland, South East Wales, north of Bristol

Environment

Support for poss EU emissions trading from 2008

Stress on minimising noise nuisance

No increase in air passenger duty

Stated aim of balancing economic growth with environmental and social factors

tion of England lived within a 50-mile (80km) radius of Manchester.

In Scotland, a new runway was preferred at Edinburgh over one at Glasgow International. A key reason was that Edinburgh was expected to remain the focus of express freight and flown mail into Scotland. Glasgow was to have substantial terminal development, which with other developments would allow growth to be accommodated "under even the most *optimistic* [emphasis added] of forecast scenarios".

However, the need for another runway might arise towards the end of the plan period (ie, by 2030), and land should be reserved. There was likely to be "little pressure to develop land north of the airport, which might be needed for a second runway at Glasgow Airport, because of existing land use and ecological designations".

The Future of Air Transport gave the aviation industry almost everything it wanted, although not always as soon as it would have liked. The third runway at Heathrow was not envisaged until 2015 at the earliest. The extra runway is important for British Airways, allowing it to maintain Heathrow as the UK's only national hub airport. BAA, the operator of Heathrow, Stansted and Gatwick airports, even got a sixth terminal at Heathrow despite the bitter battles over Terminals 4 and 5.

An ebullient Rod Eddington, British Airways chief executive, said: "For the first time, we have an effective forward-looking aviation policy which recognises Heathrow's key role as Britain's main gateway airport.

"Its continuing development has been guaranteed with Terminal Five, the opportunity to introduce mixed mode in peak periods and a third runway with a dedicated terminal. That is excellent news for the aviation industry, customers, national and regional businesses and tourism.

"We will work with the government and local authorities to establish an immediate programme of action that addresses the environmental issues at Heathrow, and we will play a full part in ensuring that these issues are resolved."

(In *mixed mode* operation planes take off and land on the same runway. Heathrow uses separate runways for takeoff and landing, and swaps these movements between the runways – *runway alternation* – to reduce disturbance to local residents.)

Mike Clasper, BAA chief executive, commented: "Aviation is vital to the economic and social wellbeing of the UK, and we are pleased that the government has taken such a long-sighted, strategic view in this white paper."

The airport operator would press ahead with plans for a second runway at Stansted, addressing local community concerns "as sympathetically as possible". BAA would also work urgently to resolve the air pollution issues at Heathrow.

Clasper said BAA was strongly committed to balancing aviation growth with measures to ensure that those who fly meet the full environmental costs of flying.

For green groups the DfT's elaborate consultation, which attracted around half a million responses, might hardly have happened. The greens agreed that the environmental measures in the white paper were nowhere near enough.

Friends of the Earth accused the government of abdicating its environmental responsibilities by giving the green light to a massive expansion in air travel. It dismissed the white paper's environmental measures as "window-dressing", and predicted that they would have minimal impact on reducing damage from the expected increase in flights.

The plans had "plunged into jeopardy" the government's long-term target to reduce greenhouse gas emissions, particularly since the release of carbon dioxide (the main greenhouse gas) from aircraft is three times as damaging as the same amount of CO_2 released at ground level.

Tony Juniper, the FOE director, said: "The aviation white paper is worse than we feared. The government has sacrificed its environmental responsibilities to satisfy the demands of the aviation industry. Alistair Darling's decision to massively expand aviation will not only be felt by people living near airports, it will affect people worldwide and impact heavily on generations yet to come."

Stephen Joseph, director of Transport 2000, said: "We've heard a few warm words on the environment but little more than that. The industry certainly hasn't been given the cold shower it needed to bring it into reality. This was the government's big opportunity to dampen down demand for aviation and bring its environmental and social problems under control, but it hasn't taken it."

T2000 welcomed the principle that aviation should pay for its environmental and social impacts, but pointed out that no framework was announced for making this actually happen.

The group said UK aviation enjoys tax concessions of around £9 billion a year, including no tax on fuel and no VAT.

The Campaign to Protect Rural England said that in the long term the white paper was "set to land a disaster on our countryside". Local environmental damage was to be controlled through mitigation and compensation, but the growth of aviation would be allowed to continue unchecked.

The CPRE supported emissions trading in order to combat climate change, but pointed out that this depended on complex and uncertain international negotiations and would take years to introduce. With no interim measures in the short term, countryside and communities "will continue to suffer from this go-for-growth approach".

Andrew Critchell, CPRE's aviation campaigner, said: "The white paper is fundamentally flawed in its failure to address the need to manage and reduce future levels of growth. Why can't the government understand the direct link between allowing continued massive growth in air transport and the onset of environmental and social problems such as the further loss of the tranquillity of the countryside and damaging climate change?"

While the green groups got little joy from the consultation, the two most prominent local campaign groups – Stop Stansted Expansion and HACAN Clear Skies (for Heathrow) – were among the biggest losers from the consultation process. Both vowed to fight on against the runways announced in the white paper.

HACAN ClearSkies said the people of London and the Thames Valley would suffer "years of uncertainty" because of the government's refusal to rule out a third runway at Heathrow. The houses that would make way for the third runway would remain blighted.

John Stewart, the HACAN chair, also expressed dismay at the prospect of mixed mode runway operation. "The threat to end runway alternation in West London will cause fury amongst local people. It is the only thing that makes life bearable for them.

"It will also be a betrayal of the government's promise that flight numbers at the airport would not exceed 480,000 a year."

Stewart reiterated that no new runways would be needed in the UK if the aviation industry's £9 billion a year tax concessions were removed.

Norman Mead, the Stop Stansted Expansion chairman, came out fighting. "The idea of a second Stansted runway is illogical and undeliverable," he said. "The government's 'green' credentials are now totally discredited by this white paper whose clear message is 'To hell with protecting the environment, our national heritage and local communities: planes take priority'. Well, we'll see about that!"

Stop Stansted Expansion said it was committed to pursuing "a vigorous and relentless challenge" to the second runway. This would include legal, regulatory and planning approaches, notably with British and European courts and authorities as well as the European Commission.

It is clear that the government's plans for British aviation are only the beginning of battles that will last for years. The white paper was not just for Christmas but for the lives of many of those involved with the runways controversy.

FIVE
UP HIGH AND PERSONAL

WHILE airline travel is expected to keep on growing, the expansion of personal air travel is set to affect our lives even more. For as long as the laisser faire paradigm holds sway, the sky is emphatically not the limit. In stage one an increasing section of the well-to-do will enjoy unparallelled personal mobility with some downside to themselves and much disturbance to the rest of us. Often these flyers will be taking to the air solely to beat the congestion on the ground. In stage two almost everyone will enjoy that mobility, but with such downside to ourselves and society that belatedly the price will seem too high.

Stage one is already well under way. To see tomorrow we must look at America now. In Medina, the billionaires' haven near Seattle favoured by Microsoft founder Bill Gates, at least one seaplane was to be seen tied up at the pier of each mega-home edging Lake Washington. The Medina authorities planned to ban helicopter pads but to allow seaplanes. (They also wanted to crack down on private tramways between the big houses and the lakeshore.)

Residents living around Van Nuys airfield in Hollywood were angered by the noise of private jets used by film stars including John Travolta, Tom Cruise and Arnold Schwarzenegger. But they failed to persuade Los Angeles City Council, which allowed operations at least until 2010.

The residents of exclusive Aspen in the Rocky

Mountains are well aware of how aircraft noise can destroy the mountain idyll. The magazine Aircraft Illustrated on a visit to the town in 2000 reported that Aspen Pitkin County Airport had some of the strictest noise regulations of any airport in North America. Restrictions included a flights curfew and a required "high approach" to runway 33 (one of two runways) without overflying the town. The airport authority also urged pilots to use minimum reverse thrust when landing, "in response to the local community and environmental concerns". Nevertheless, the skies around Aspen sounded to considerably more than birdsong. In latest figures available to the magazine, there were 43,320 movements at Aspen Pitkin County Airport in 1998 – an average of 119 movements a day. Almost two-thirds of these movements (over 27,500) were by business aircraft, many no doubt being used by rich residents who balked at the tough 160-mile (260km) road journey to Denver. The residents were directly contributing to the nuisance that through airport regulations they sought to reduce – an example of the inconsistency to which we are all prone in our uses of transport.

The National Business Aviation Association (in the US) found that company managers using their own jets for business travel increased from 56 per cent to 72 per cent in the two years to 2001. Three hundred of the 500 top American companies, appearing in the Fortune 500 list, owned a corporate jet.

If anyone is entitled to a private jet, that is surely plane-maker Boeing. In the mid-Nineties, the Mail on Sunday reported approvingly, Boeing "ran only three small corporate jets". Among the "excesses" of Phil Condit, the chief executive who resigned suddenly in late 2003, was "a fleet of jets, including a 737 fitted out for Condit in the style of an English library".

The United States had 219,464 active aircraft in its

general (non-military) aviation fleet in 1999, according to Federal Aviation Administration figures. Only 4,138 were for "public use" (airliners), and 4,279 were air taxis. At least 83 per cent of the fleet was for private flying: 10,804 listed as corporate, 24,543 business and 147,085 personal. Piston engines predominated with 171,923 aircraft; there were 12,799 turboprops or turbojets, 7,448 rotary craft, 2,041 gliders and 4,725 lighter-than-air craft. Shades of the Wright Brothers were invoked with 20,528 "experimental" aircraft, most of these being amateur.

Sao Paulo, Brazil's overgrown business capital with a population of 17 million, illustrates all too clearly the interface between congestion on the ground and growing use of the air. The pilots' association claimed that more private helicopter flights were made there than anywhere in the world. The number of helicopters was said to have quadrupled to 450 in the six years to 2000. Choppers made 2,000 landings for a Formula One race event that year while landings on Avenida Paulista, the city's main business street, averaged about 80 a day.

Fabrice Cagnat, commercial director for a helicopter firm, said sweepingly if understandably, disregarding about 99.8 per cent of city residents: "Having a helicopter is not only accepted here but it is considered a necessary tool for existing."

Europe has been slower than America to take up corporate jets, traditionally seeing them as a mark of extravagance. But US investor Warren Buffett, who was in Britain in 2001 to promote his corporate jet company NetJet, said: "I can't conceive of a Europe without thousands of owners [with some sharing planes] 10 years from now." At that time there were about 2,000 corporate jets in operation across Europe.

The UK register of civil aircraft, maintained by the Civil Aviation Authority, contained just over 16,500

current registrations at November 1, 2002. Most were
fixed-wing aircraft (59 per cent); there were 3,623
microlights, 1,807 balloons and 1,130 helicopters. The
total of registered aircraft has been growing slowly,
but even so has increased by two-thirds since 1985,
when there were fewer than 10,000 current registrations. Helicopters have more than doubled in number,
from 522 in 1985. So have microlights, from 1,579 at
the earlier date.

Aircraft registrations in Britain are proportionately
(adjusting for the population difference) less than half
those of the United States, indicating the potential for
further growth. The total of 16,500 aircraft compares
with the same number of car registrations in Britain
in 1905 – and look what happened then!

Philip Green, boss of the Arcadia fashion group which
owns many British household name brands, took Kate
Rankine on an assignment for the Daily Telegraph for a
ride in his six-seater Lear jet. At 30,000ft (9,100m) over
the French Alps, Rankine reported, the entrepreneur
relaxed with his stockinged feet on the mushroom-
coloured seat and commented: "It's very civilised up
here, isn't it?" And so it is for those in the plane. Less so
for those on the ground. Far less so as corporate jets
become increasingly common.

The Royal Commission on Environmental Pollution,
in a special report directed at the British government's
consultation on airport expansion, reserved some of its
strongest words for the global prospect of supersonic
business jets typically carrying eight to 10 passengers.
Aircraft in the stratosphere are a threat to ozone levels, which protect the earth from excessive solar radiation. "The contribution to global climate change of
this kind of aircraft [supersonic corporate jets] would
be so disproportionate that their development and promotion must be regarded as grossly irresponsible," the
commission said.

In Britain, the age of the air taxi came closer when Richard Noble announced a plan to use 250 small airfields dotted around Britain for his projected Farnborough F1, a six-seat single-engined turboprop which would be able to land on 2,600ft (790m) runways – barely half the length of runway used by the bigger commercial flights.

Noble is the man behind Thrust, the car which broke the sound barrier in the Nevada desert in 1997 and had to be driven carefully to prevent it taking off. He saw his plan to use the airstrips, many of them built during the Second World War, as the answer to increasingly congested airports. "In Britain you're never further than 20 minutes away from an airfield which can handle the F1," he enthused in words to chill lovers of peace and quiet in the countryside.

As will the idea of an aircraft with operating costs per mile "projected to be similar to an executive car, bringing affordable personalised travel at speeds of up to 400mph [640kph] to a segment of air travellers for who business jets are out of viable economic reach", to quote Farnborough Aircraft Corporation Ltd. Noble's project ran into problems, but the vision lives on. The new management expects the F1 to achieve European and US certification by 2006.

The company explained that the all-composite airframe was designed for volume production, and the F1 would be suitable for charter operators, air taxi work and business flying. The plane was intended to sell for $2m (£1.2m).

The issues raised by private flying are the familiar ones of noise, pollution and safety, to which must be added privacy. The private helicopter is surely the most anti-social of all forms of transport. Its noisy passage across the sky disturbs thousands at a time for the sake of one person's convenience. The Council for the Protection of Rural England (CPRE) formally put the difficulties to government when it spoke of "increasing concern about the extreme disturbance caused by helicopters in both private and commercial service flying from small airfields and between larger airports". It pointed out that leisure flying (unlike commercial flying) is not restricted for noise and its impact on rural tranquillity.

Oxford airport is popular with learner pilots, who can often be seen – and heard – doing circuits and bumps above the surrounding countryside. In a letter to the (London) Independent, Robin Alden of Oxford took up the cudgels on behalf of residents living near smaller (non-designated) airports like Oxford and Redhill, Surrey, used by light aircraft, helicopters and business jets. "Why is it that neither our UK nor EU legislators have so far paid any attention to the noise nuisance created by so-called non-designated airports which service general aviation... ?" he asked. "Will Alistair Darling [the transport secretary] and his junior ministers please answer this question, instead of persistently ignoring it?"

If private flying is troubling residents around Britain's smaller airports, it's nothing to what they can expect in future.

England does not have a law against invasion of privacy, but judicial decisions under the 1998 Human Rights Act may create one piece by piece. The two private citizens in the lawsuit to include Gatwick in the government's airport consultation (see Chapter Three) based their action in part on the HRA Article 8 (1) (respect for private life, home and correspondence) and Article 1 of the First Protocol (peaceful enjoyment of possessions). This part of their claim failed, but Mr Justice Kay's reasons for rejection are of interest. What was taking place was simply a consultation with a view to framing national policy: "no authorisation or permission has been given, or is for determination, which can be said to interfere with the Article 8 rights ... Nor is it inevitable that such authorisation or permission will be given." The judge also held that any disadvantage to the claimants, who were both from the Stansted area, "derives not from the exclusion of Gatwick from the options but from the inclusion of Stansted, which noone is suggesting to be unlawful in any way".

The First Protocol claim was refused for similar reasons. Perhaps, however, if the case had been about a solid proposal rather than one possibility among several, the outcome might have been different.

Helicopters, microlights and aircraft types yet unknown will be far more of an invasion of privacy than airliners and executive jets because they fly lower. From dukes to dustcart drivers all will be equal in loss of seclusion. The biggest estates, and city parks, will be as overlooked as the back garden of a London terrace house. Lovers will draw apart, naturists will give up their sun worship and tea parties on the lawn will be burdened by uninvited onlookers. We will reverse the science fiction visions of mega-cities surrounded by an unvisited and sometimes prohibited great outdoors. We will flee to the great indoors of our rooms to get away from it all.

The consequences of aerial accidents are vastly greater than for land accidents, compounded by the further risk to those on the ground underneath. Even the simple act of running out of fuel is more than an irritation. Because of this higher standards' of operation, maintenance and readiness are required for private pilots than for private motorists.

We have seen, however, that drivers' behaviour is marked by an acceptance of risk and a casual approach to safety. As planes become an everyday reality like a car, the same approach is likely to prevail in the air as on the ground. Nor will there be minimal use of a private plane, reserved for Sunday outings or special needs. From motor cars to mobile phones, an item once acquired is used widely in order to justify the outlay and the decision to buy.

A 10-year-old boy, Laurence Hughes, died in a midair collision when he was having a flying lesson. The Cessna 152 and a Russian-built Yak replica warplane hit each other over Essex. The two others aboard the two planes were also killed. Although it was not clear whether Laurence or his instructor was at the controls at the time, it was not disputed that the boy was having a flying lesson. Indeed, the boy's father seemed proud of the fact. Robin Hughes, the Daily Telegraph reported, said: "Laurence was only 10 but he lived for flying. He spent all his spare time building and flying planes." Mr Hughes went on: "Andy Duffill [the instructor] was our best friend. He taught me to fly and taught our sons, Laurence, and his brother Elliott [even younger than Laurence]."

As reported by the newspaper, Mr Hughes's statement did not address the question of the appropriateness of a 10-year-old learning to fly. With incalculably higher stakes, it is the same parental impulse, translated to the air, that is seen in thousands of private tracks, driveways and abandoned airstrips where children learn to drive cars. To the adult such precosity may seem amusing or a source of macho pride, but the act of pleasing the child can have tragic results, as the case of Laurence Hughes sadly shows.

In the early days of motoring a despairing E.M. Forster foresaw cars swarming everywhere. He gave it 50 years, and has been proved on the mark. He saw the same thing happening in the air. He has not been proved wrong; merely not right yet. It is perhaps surprising that it hasn't yet happened in the air. The centenary of the world's first powered and controlled flight (by the Wright Brothers) fell in 2003 so the aeroplane is almost as old as the motor car.

Peter Thorold, in *The Motoring Age* (Profile Books, 2003) makes clear that as early as 1923 it "became understood, particularly among the young, that the car was merely a forerunner, and that the future of passenger transport, except perhaps for short runs, lay with the helicopter and light aircraft".

Richard Noble's 250 airfields around Britain may spawn an expansion of light aircraft use, but stage two in the growth of personal flying will be truly underway when operations are liberated from airstrips and landing pads. A determined attempt to create a personal flying machine was announced by Millennium Jet of California with its SoloTrek XFV (for eXoskeletor Flying Vehicle). Disbelief at the practicalities of the device was tempered by the information that Nasa was taking an interest for its possible military applications. US military interest in personal flying vehicles goes back at least to the Vietnam war.

With the SoloTrek the operator will travel standing up, secured to a framework and with two counter-rotating ducted fans for propulsion above the head. This position was said to be as comfortable as being wrapped in a friendly bear hug – that is, very comfortable. The machine is planned to reach up to 80mph (130kph) with a range of about 150 miles (240km) on a tank of ordinary pump petrol. The operator will simply walk in, strap up and lift off – up to 9,000ft (2,700m), although reassuringly a parachute will be included among the SoloTrek's array of hi-tech safety features.

The developers were keen to stress the safety of the machine. It will not become enabled until the operator has programmed in his or her correct weight. Sensors will detect any developing problems with life-critical systems or components, or with fuel supply. An overpowered engine with all appropriate backups will give the operator peace of mind while a global positioning system will help him to navigate and avoid collisions.

Personal flying machines have some way to go before they displace the 7.15 train to the office. The ingenious SoloTrek has obvious possibilities for sport flying and presumably for military use, but for general use would be restricted by wind and weather. In sci-fi films it is usually a clear, windless day but the real elements are not so welcoming. The vision of hundreds of flyers buzzing around the City of London and Wall Street business districts with the same gusto that they currently bring to driving their Porsches and Astons suggests a brisk trade in hospital casualty departments and morgues. Many victims of these collisions would be on the ground.

The same limitations apply to microlights, which no doubt is why fewer than 4,000 are registered in Britain. Timandra Harkness was an enthusiastic user of one of them. She wrote about the experience in the Daily Telegraph: "You can have the same freedom of the air as you do on the ground – arguably more since nobody will do you for speeding at 3,000ft [910m] and you are unlikely to meet a taxi doing a U-turn." Easy to imagine the early motorists saying the same sort of thing. Sadly, such freedom is temporary and vanishes as more people flood in to enjoy it – encouraged by breathless newspaper articles.

Flying cars would have to be as easy to use as the family Ford, and big and powerful enough to cope with the weather. Hollywood's favourite way of announcing the future is a realistic prospect for Sir Clive Sinclair, the pioneer of personal computers and a visionary inventor whose testimony should not be disregarded. He told the BBC-TV programme Tomorrow's World in 1999 that the technology of flying cars would be available in 10 years, although the "infrastructure" would take longer.

Sinclair hoped to be one of the pioneers. He unveiled his plans to the Sunday Times, saying: "I've been thinking about this for years, but it's just recently that new technology has made it economically possible. Once these things are being built they will become as cheap to buy as a family car."

The Sinclair flying car would have fins but no wings, relying on a curved roof and flat underbody to sustain flight. The vertical takeoff craft would be powered by hydrogen fuel cells and have a range of 500 miles (800km) and a top speed of 200mph (320kph). It would be no longer than the typical family car and about half the length of an average light aircraft.

Sinclair remarked: "Clearly, you would not want people like me flying them so it will have to be controlled by a [satellite] navigation system." The system would fly the car automatically to its destination, although the driver would take control in an emergency.

For all but the scifi enthusiast the vision of flying cars proceeding in an orderly way may be more appealing than that of individually operated cars buzzing anarchically here and there, Hollywood-style. But is that really where it ends? If the driver can decide to take control in an emergency, what is to stop the boy racer taking over in a non-emergency just for the hell of it? (For acceptable safety standards the driver must always be able to override the machine. The system or vehicle that decides its own emergency might find that the breakdown prevents control being passed to the driver.)

All infrastructure systems break down at some point; the potential consequences of highways in the sky doing so are particularly severe. Or at least they seem so today. We may find a coarsening of the moral sensibility leads us to accept a certain number of deaths from vehicles falling out of the sky as an acceptable price for convenience, as we have done on the roads.

The technology to create a flying car, although formidable, is the least of the problems facing sexagenarian Sir Clive. The good news for conservationists is that down to earth issues like insurance and finance are likely to stymie the project in the near future. If it is hard to obtain affordable insurance for a sports car, insurance for a flying car is barely imaginable. This is particularly so given the risk to bystanders and passers-by: public liability insurance premiums across the board soared after the September 11 2001 terror attacks in the United States.

Investment funding to create the infrastructure for flying cars would be wildly speculative, and that isn't the way grand scale projects are put together. It is hard to see a government that cannot afford to rehabilitate the London Tube becoming involved, while private capital would shy from unknowable prospects. Tarred roads were not essential for the early motor cars, but flying cars in the form envisaged by Sinclair need elaborate infrastructure to operate. Few if any would buy the cars without the certainty of being able to use them, but without the certainty of a user base who would invest in the infrastructure?

To say, however, that these difficulties mean flying cars will never happen is to subscribe to a 1910-type myth: it is like saying that motor cars would never catch on because there were few decent roads to run them on.

Sir Clive Sinclair is not alone in his dreams. Nasa's Morphing Project, looking at aerospace technology around 2020, foresaw a personal air car. This would carry four passengers at up to 400mph (640kph), and take off and land vertically.

A vision of flying cars was offered by Sussex University's mechanical engineering department – and it was a Frisbee. A large Frisbee-like disc would be mounted on the car to act like a wing in flight and for use in takeoffs and landings. For takeoff the Frisbee would give lift and for landing it would provide drag, with the vehicle "feathering down like a sycamore seed", according to Dr Alan Turner from Sussex.

The quietness of the flying car as foreseen by Dr Turner would be a boon compared to the noisiness of a helicopter. Appearance, however, would take getting used to: a massive disc of 13-13 3/4 ft (4-4.2m) would be needed for a lightweight car.

Dutch designers came out with what seems the simplest flying car of all – an "Autocopter" that flies like a helicopter and on the ground becomes a car by folding away its rotor blades. This must-have item for the suburban commuter was expected to be on the market in 2006 at around £50,000.

The prospect of Man taking to the air as readily as he once took to the roads will excite some and appal others. Many will question whether it will happen in the way suggested here. After all, aircraft have been around almost as long as the car. When Orville Wright made the world's first powered and controlled flight (lasting 12 seconds) in 1903, motoring was in its infancy. It was less than 20 years since Karl Benz and Gottlieb Daimler produced the first practical horseless carriages. The legendary Model T Ford, which revolutionised the world's motor industry with its 15 million production run, was five years into the future.

H.J. Dyos and D.H. Aldcroft*, explaining the early years in Britain, say the economics of the two industries were quite different. The motor vehicle found a large and growing demand for surface transport that

---

* *British Transport: An Economic Survey from the Seventeenth Century to the Twentieth* (Penguin Books, 1974. First published by Leicester University Press, 1969)

it could easily tap. The aeroplane had little in its favour except speed: the early aircraft were very inefficient with low capacity and high maintenance charges; people distrusted what they felt was a dangerous mode of travel.

"There were no fortunes to be made in aviation as there were in developing motor transport," the authors remark. The difficulties were long-lasting: "Few if any British air operators ever made a real profit in the interwar years." The government had to come to the rescue in 1921 after the four pioneering air companies were unable to continue operations. Six companies, including two French ones, had been working the London-Paris route, but it was "inconceivable" that the route could support that number.

Although many routes have been persistently uneconomic up to the present, the aviation industry's situation overall was transformed after the Second World War. A mass market for foreign holidays emerged, and the internationalisation of business meant a huge rise in this type of travel. The expansion of Western economics has left business leaders with the means and the appetite for corporate jets, while technology is bringing the prospect of personal air travel in forms barely imagined.

Aviation's growth record is there for all to see. The expected huge expansion of airline travel will add layers of disturbance to our lives, with health and safety implications and the destruction of homes and countryside for more airport capacity. Business and hobby flying increasingly will mean benefits for some to the disbenefit of all. Writer Sir John Mortimer must fear ever-worsening experiences over his country retreat when already on Sunday afternoons, as he lamented in the Daily Mail, "every spare-time pilot criss-crosses the sky, practising looping the loop, being careful only to avoid the helicopters which are buzzing furiously, transporting weekend guests to the stately homes of various television personalities".

Beyond this, serious scientists expect personal flying vehicles to become a reality, putting the stuff of sci-fi stories and Hollywood fantasies on the edge of achievement. Of course it is Man's destiny to invent and explore. It is exciting to work at the leading edge of technology. Driving and flying are enjoyable activities. Cars and planes have turned travel from the pastime of the rich to a commonplace for all. With a trip to the countryside or to another country, travel has broadened the horizons of millions; even allowed their humanity to blossom from a formerly stunted domestic environment. None of this should be denied. However, the heedless expansion of air travel will bring us a future we don't want, and it will have happened by accident.

In the end it's up to us. Politicians will not move ahead of public opinion on such a major issue. We need to ask ourselves some big questions, including travel for what? The average length of car journeys in Britain is increasing all the time. There is a suggestion here of travel for its own sake. Travel becomes an addiction, an end rather than a means. Of course we dress our wanderings up with reasons: a holiday, a cultural tour, a sporting event, a meeting, a visit to family or friends. But do we need to go so far, so often, so quickly?

Cars and planes encourage an "if it's Tuesday this must be Belgium" approach to travel – a cathedral in an hour, a town in a morning, a country in a day. These places are worth far more. By visiting fewer places we would enjoy them more, and we would cut down our travel.

Visitors from 1910 might be less impressed than we are by our ability to drive from London to Liverpool and back in a day. They would notice instead the shocking price at which this has been bought: sprawling towns, polluted air, deaths at high speed, a culture of isolation, noise everywhere. They would be horrified by the prospect of it happening again in the air. This is the "1910 effect". If we could go back to their time, when there were 53,000 cars registered in Britain (there are now more than 27 million), would we say carry on regardless? So where do we want to go from here with the skies?

SIX
SUMMARY – TIME TO
CHOOSE

THE announcement in the summer of 2002 – just when many of us were jetting off for our holidays – that demand for air travel in Britain was set almost to treble by 2030 was shocking in the literal sense. With unavoidable evidence of climate change and aviation's role in it, a massive increase is flying seemed profoundly wrong. There were common-sense fears, despite official denials, that you cannot put more and more planes into already crowded skies without compromising safety. For the hundreds of thousands, or millions, who are troubled by aircraft noise the last news they needed was to expect even more of the same. Those not already afflicted might wonder if it will be their turn next.

The likely growth of air freight was even more shocking, although it failed to grab the headlines. It was expected to grow more than sixfold, and because of the need for next-day deliveries – much of the raison d'etre for air freight – many more night flights will be required.

Bigger planes and quieter planes can take the edge off the raw statistics – points the aviation industry is sure to stress. But the respected Royal Commission on Environmental Pollution believes the effect of technological fixes will be outstripped by growth of traffic. It chillingly observed that two-thirds of the aircraft which will be flying in 2030 are already in use (and, therefore, most of the world's stock has limited scope to benefit from technological improvements).

Predictions for passengers and freight are if growth is "unconstrained". In other words it is not inevitable. But in December 2003 it became more likely with the Department for Transport's white paper, *The Future of Air Transport*. Although the department shies away from the term, this was a classic "predict and provide" exercise. It took the high scenario of airport usage and looked for ways to meet it with a capacity of 470 million passengers per annum. If carried into effect, this would mean at least four new runways, including two in the already crowded South East, with new terminals and other expansion around the country.

The government expressed awareness of the environmental and social impacts of this massive increase in flying, but clearly viewed aviation's benefits to the economy as paramount. Yet these benefits are by no means as clearcut as industry boosters would have us believe. We need only think of huge and growing deficit on Britain's tourism account because the money flies away with the holidaymakers, or the jobs lost here because manufacturing and agriculture have migrated and the products sent back by air freight.

The air industry is said to support directly 200,000 jobs and indirectly up to three times as many more. The point is a red herring in terms of aviation expansion. Who is asking for these jobs to be abolished or for the aviation sector to shrink? However, against a background where good jobs go unfilled all over the country we can certainly challenge the idea that its job-producing capacity is a reason for expanding the sector.

The alternative to the effectively limitless growth of flying accepted by the DfT is the management of demand. Some of the ways are described in this book. Demand management is not about stopping people flying, but it is about encouraging people not to fly *more*.

It is hard to argue that we do not have enough flying opportunities already. Most air trips are for social and leisure purposes. A balance needs to be found between these and the interests of the residents on the ground. Who are these residents? They are all of us. The argument of this essay is that aviation is where motoring was in 1910. Around then was the last chance to arrange the growth of motor transport in socially benign ways. As it was, growth was unconstrained for decades. When the downsides of traffic at existing levels became apparent, it was far too late to do anything about it. Attempts by recent governments have been like trying to hold the tide back with a saucepan, and inevitably these have failed: road traffic in Britain is still growing, and the present government has done a U-turn with its programme to expand the motorway system.

As a nation we have set out on the same course in the air, with less good reason than our forebears had with motoring since the upsides and downsides of aviation are there for all to see.

It may be that the public are ahead of the Department for Transport in being ready to accept limits to growth, weighing cheap flights against our deeper interests in safe journeys, quiet skies and a healthy planet.

The same consensual approach offers the only prospect of returning sanity to the roads, remote as that is. The array of technical measures like road pricing, congestion charges, speed cameras, speed bumps, chicanes, alternate flow points, pedestrianised streets, road painting, rumble strips, prohibited turns, traffic lights and roundabouts are all attempts to button down the unbuttonable. The only ultimate solution is a change of attitude, when we simply accept to use our cars less. Some practical ways are suggested in the ladder of substitution in Chapter Two.

In fact, we are using our cars more: the average journey length in Britain is still increasing. For everyone's sake we should try to halt this trend, which seems to contain elements of travel for its own sake. In so far as these increasing journey lengths are made up of leisure visits, the car frequently degrades the tourism experience by tempting us to fit in too much – a cathedral in an hour, a town in a morning, a country in a day. This compulsive movement, translated into the air, does not bode well for our turbulent skies if mass travel becomes even more available and personal flying becomes commonplace.

This essay is about more than the growth of public air transport, just as the story of motoring is about more than buses. Private flying is not huge in Britain – there were just over 16,500 civil aircraft of all sorts registered in late-2002 – but it has been growing steadily. Since 1985 numbers have increased by two-thirds. Also, small planes and helicopters cause aggravation out of all proportion to their numbers, so the prospect of more to come will be deeply unwelcome to many on the ground.

Further ahead, flying cars offering mobility for Mr and Mrs Ordinary are better left on the Hollywood cinema screen than brought to our communities. Yet such vehicles are taken seriously by some scientists including Sir Clive Sinclair, the innovatory entrepreneur whose opinions should not be dismissed. Sir Clive said in 1999 that the technology for the flying car would exist in 10 years' time although the infrastructure would take longer.

The idea of flying cars has been around for a century so why should we give any thought to it? For most of that time it was simply a fantasy; now it is a technology waiting to be born. Nor could the project happen without enough rich people to form a user base. Now the emerging technology may unite with the affluence of Western societies to make the product feasible. After that the flying car will await its Henry Ford.

The inspiration of the original Henry Ford and his followers means there is scarcely a lane in the deepest countryside of Britain that cannot expect its regular daily motor traffic. Away from the roads we can enjoy visual privacy even though the noise may continue. Moving in three dimensions, the flying car will strip away the last of our privacy. It will also raise safety, noise and pollution issues, as its land-based counterpart does. We don't know when but we can see it coming: happy new year, 1910!

INDEX